Assertive- Responsive Management

A Personal Handbook

Malcolm E. Shaw

Educational Systems and Designs, Inc.

Addison-Wesley

Publishing Company

Reading, Massachusetts
Menlo Park, California
London · Amsterdam
Don Mills, Ontario · Sydney

ISBN 0-201-06819-2
ABCDEFGHIJ-AL-79

Preface

Getting things done. You get things done in organizations by influencing other people. You influence other people by interacting with them. This book is designed to present a comprehensive review of the modes of inter-action that are available to you as you work with others to establish direction and achieve results.

The concepts, strategies, and methods that are outlined in each chapter are built on the premise that *everyone* can improve. You can identify and capital-ize upon your strengths. You can identify your liabilities and either convert them to positive resources or develop the capacities and skills required to overcome them. Step by step procedures for assessing and improving your leadership behavior are covered in sequence, chapter by chapter.

Chapter 1. Your leadership behavior. Taking inventory. The first step in improving anything is to know where you stand. Chapter 1 provides you with an oppor-tunity to take a quick look at your present behavior. You complete a ques-tionnaire that has been used by thousands of managers. You are to compare your basic leadership approach with others'. The process of determining where you stand and how effective you are is the concern of each of the chapters.

Chapter 2. A leadership model. The next step in the self-improvement process is to be aware of the alternatives that are available to you. A leadership model that outlines those alternatives is presented. Aggressive, Assertive, Respon-sive, and Nonassertive patterns of behavior are defined.

Chapter 3. Where are you? Where do you choose to be? By assessing your present behavior, by becoming more aware of the options available to you, and by then reviewing practical experience and research regarding leadership be-havior, you can determine more specifically your personal effectiveness goals and begin to define how to achieve them. There is usually some gap between where you are and where you want to be. Chapter 3 aids you in

iii

defining this gap and determining where you choose to be. A Planning and Development Guide is provided to help you focus on specific goals and the behavior required to reach them.

Chapter 4. The leadership model. Specific patterns of behavior. As you determine how to be more effective as a leader or organizational member, it becomes necessary to pin down patterns of behavior that are available to you. Chapter 4 identifies the basic characteristics of leadership and demonstrates leadership patterns.

Chapter 5. Getting in touch with your feelings. Many managers try to improve their techniques and change certain aspects of their own behavior mostly on an intellectual basis. The fact is that in large measure your actions are a function of your feelings. Your feelings are a major resource in moving from where you are to where you want to be. However, in order for your emotions to be useful to you, it is essential for you to be in touch with those emotions. Chapter 5 provides you with an opportunity to identify and get in closer touch with your emotional resources *and* begin to use these resources as energizers for action.

Chapter 6. Becoming more Assertive. Most managers want to improve their ability to have impact on others and to influence events; they want to work with individuals in ways that build respect and trust and that contribute to the achievement of personal and organizational purpose. For most people this means that they must move increasingly in the direction of Assertive behavior—expressing themselves, having impact on people without turning them off or creating undue resistance or hostility. In order to move in a more Assertive direction some individuals need to overcome their own timidity; others need to overcome their inappropriately dominating or Aggressive behavior. In either case, knowledge of Assertive strategies and techniques is useful. Practice in the application of Assertive skills makes a direct contribution to personal effectiveness. This chapter deals with becoming more Assertive.

Chapter 7. Becoming more Responsive. A great deal of current literature and practice in leadership and management behavior emphasizes influencing other people, being Assertive, and providing direction for others. Than emphasis has been extended in popular literature to a growing concern with "Number One." Most experienced managers know—and research confirms—that in order to achieve organizational purpose and self-fulfillment one must draw upon the resources of others and engage them in tasks in ways that enhance their creativity, self-fulfillment, and commitment. Therefore attention must be paid to drawing out the influence and resources of others, and to being available, responsive, and supportive in the development of collaborative and cooperative relationships. This often overlooked dimension of leadership effectiveness is the focus of this chapter and involves increasing your knowledge and skill in being Responsive.

Ways of developing specific Responsive techniques—listening skills, processes for engaging others and for increasing your own openness and awareness of the needs and goals of others—are provided.

Chapters 8 and 9. Becoming more Assertive and Responsive. Practice. In learning to speak a language, to play a musical instrument, or to improve a physical skill, you expect to practice regularly and rigorously. Until recently, leadership skills have rarely been rehearsed or practiced in the same kind of systematic way that golfing, basketball, speech, and musical instruments are practiced. Chapters 8 and 9 provide frameworks for practicing and applying Assertive and Responsive behavior. In addition, specific models—step-by-step procedures—are presented for setting goals, reviewing performance, and (in Chapter 9) resolving conflict. These models provide a framework for practicing Assertive-Responsive skills while also illustrating three important leadership functions. Setting goals is at the core of leadership because it involves establishing direction for personal and organizational growth. Reviewing and improving performance—keeping operations on the track—are critical to maintaining or redefining direction. And throughout every phase of organizational life conflict—inevitable, necessary human disagreement—is the ubiquitous ingredient that leaders must face and resolve if they and their organizations are to survive.

Chapter 10. The future. In order to move from where you are to where you want to be, it is important to be clear about the consequences of your own actions; and, especially, to develop, clarify, and act upon a system of beliefs which is fulfilling, effective, and socially valid. This chapter aids you in reviewing your beliefs and values and contrasting these values implicit in your actions.

Putting it together. Although each chapter of this book moves through a step-by-step approach to leadership effectiveness, organizational life is rarely ordered and sequential. Organization members live and work in an environment that is often unpredictable and at times hostile. Within the changing framework of the organization its members are constantly faced with choices. As a leader and organization member you can choose to be dominated by its environment, that is, by the opinions, needs, and demands of others, or you can choose to ignore the environment to avoid responding to the needs, opinions, or feelings of others.

This book has been written with the conviction that effective, life-oriented leaders are capable of both acting upon the environment and responding to it. Assertive and Responsive skills and the values and beliefs that support them provide you with affirmative choices, choices that produce positive, results-oriented interactions with the world around you.

Westport, Connecticut   M. E. S.
April 1979

Acknowledgments

Wallace Wohlking of the New York State School of Industrial and Labor Relations (Cornell) first suggested that Assertiveness Training should be modified to fit the needs of managers. Cornell University sponsored the first Assertiveness Training Program for Managers.

Pearl Rutledge, Ph.D., trained the author and his associates at ESD (Educational Systems and Designs, Inc.) in Assertiveness Training (AT) techniques and contributed to the design of ESD's initial programs.

Frances LaBella of ESD has been associated with the AT program since its inception and cotrains with the author in programs conducted for the American Management Associations (AMA) and other groups. Many of the program materials have been influenced by her ideas and involvement.

Emmett Wallace, Ph.D., of ESD, has also been closely associated with the program and was involved in much of the original research in communications upon which the Leadership Model was built.

Elaine Carter, a consultant in organizational behavior and social change, participated in ESD's initial program development activities in AT and has adapted many of these techniques to specialized programs in career development and minority group affairs.

David Ryan, formerly vice-president at AMA, brought ESD's AT program to consistently growing groups of managers. Peter Biardi and Betsy Sanders, both of AMA, have extended the scope of the program. It is now offered ten times a year throughout the United States.

Long before the development of the AT program, Sonja and Michael Gilligan developed a new frame of reference and new approaches for improving personal effectiveness. Their ideas, methods, and personal insight have greatly influenced this book.

Frances Butler and Susan Powley typed the manuscript and stayed with the project through many changes and revisions.

My wife Jean contributed directly to the development of many of the concepts covered in the book, particularly the section on responsiveness.

Contents

1

Your Leadership Behavior. Taking Inventory

LEADERSHIP EFFECTIVENESS

The key to effective leadership lies in *how* you interact with others, *how* you involve others in clarifying and working toward goals, and *how* you go about influencing people and events. Can you improve your effectiveness? What is your present leadership orientation? Should you change?

To Begin

The first step in improving anything is to know how it is currently operating. The clearer you are about your current leadership behavior the better chance you have to assess it, to get in closer touch with how you are utilizing your resources, and decide what changes, if any, you want to make.

An Inventory has been designed to assist you in exploring how you actually feel and behave, not how you *should* feel and behave. It is not concerned with what you *must do* or *should do* but with what you actually do. The Inventory is designed to aid you in assessing the ways in which you utilize your resources in interacting with other organization members and the ways in which you draw upon the resources of others as you strive to get things done. The nature of the A and R behavior will be described in detail after you have had an opportunity to complete the format based on your own experiences and beliefs.

The format and instructions for the Inventory follow. As you fill out the Inventory, think in terms of your most frequent reactions, even though your behavior changes from situation to situation. In order to get the freshest, most spontaneous view of how you use your abilities, complete the Inventory before starting the next section.

A & R RESOURCES INVENTORY—YOU[1]

INSTRUCTIONS Below you will find a series of paired statements, an "A" statement and an "R" statement. You are asked to distribute 10 points between the two statements. You might give all 10 points to the A statement and no points to the R statement. This would indicate that the A statement comes *closest* to describing your behavior or feelings and the R statement is not at all descriptive. You might give equal points (5 points to A, 5 points to R) if both statements fit your behavior about equally. (You might give 8 to A and 2 to R, or 4 to A and 6 to R, and so on.) For each question, the number of points for A plus R should equal 10.

PAIRED STATEMENTS

A STATEMENTS	R STATEMENTS
1. I get things done by shaping events, by having a direct impact on people. Points _____	I get things done by "tuning in" on and responding to the people and situations around me. Points _____
2. When I am dissatisfied with an individual's performance I become more demanding with the individual. I may make suggestions or set goals for improvement. Points _____	When I am dissatisfied with an individual's performance, I observe, listen, and try to understand the individual's behavior. I try to involve him/her in setting goals. Points _____
3. If I err in dealing with poor performance it is in the direction of being abrasive or resentful. (I might be seen as angry or hostile.) Points _____	If I err in dealing with poor performance it is in the direction of being accommodating or patronizing. (I might be seen as overly tolerant and compromising.) Points _____
4. In most group situations I am one of the people who initiate ideas, suggest alternatives, and energize the process. Points _____	In most group situations I am one of the people who provide stability and balance. I respond to the ideas of others. Points _____
5. I get results by using my own energy. Points _____	I get results by tapping the energy of others. Points _____
6. I defend myself from attack or criticism by fighting back clearly and straightforwardly. I use my energy to straighten things out. Points _____	I defend myself from attack or criticism by distracting or diffusing the energy of my opponent. I let the other person tire himself or herself out. Points _____
7. If I err it is on the side of being too tough. Points _____	If I err it is on the side of being too tolerant. Points _____

8. When people disagree with one of my ideas or suggestions I tend to "speed up" and try to sell them on my approach.

Points _____

When people disagree with one of my ideas or suggestions I tend to "slow down" and consider their reservations.

Points _____

9. I put effort into being sure that people understand my point of view.

Points _____

I put effort into being sure that I understand the views of others.

Points _____

10. Under pressure my strength lies in my ability to get "fired up" and to inspire others to act.

Points _____

Under pressure my strength lies in my ability to "take in" and remain open to the feelings of others.

Points _____

11. My ability to be a strong competitor has paid off for me.

Points _____

My ability to be cooperative and to build collaborative relationships has paid off for me.

Points _____

12. In working with others I spend more time talking than listening.

Points _____

In working with others I spend more time listening than talking.

Points _____

Total A points _____

Total R points _____

INTERPRETING YOUR A AND R RESULTS

The way in which you spread points between the paired statements on the A & R Inventory provides you with information concerning your leadership behavior. The Inventory is built on the basis of the fact that you have *three* choices available to you as you work with others to set goals, solve problems, and achieve results.

1. You can *act* upon others; you can use your energy, knowledge, and power to shape outcomes, to influence others, to defend yourself, and to stand up for your rights.[2] This active, shaping behavior will be labeled A behavior. Your A score indicates the degree to which you *act* on your environment in contrast with your pattern of *reacting*.

2. You can *react* to others; you can show regard for and interest in their needs and goals; you can respond to and be influenced by their energy, knowledge, and power. This reactive, responsive behavior will be labeled R behavior. Your R score, in contrast to your A score, gives an indication of your reactive pattern.

3. You can act upon *and* react to others; you can strive to influence them and seek out and respond to their influence. You can integrate A and R behavior into an interactive, two-way influence process. This will be described as A/R behavior. By analyzing the relationship between your A and R scores you can determine your basic leadership orientation.

On balance, over time you have developed a dominant leadership style. The way in which you combine your need and desire to shape events with your need and desire to tune into and be influenced by others determines your leadership style. To aid you in clarifying your style, and subsequently contrasting it with experienced managers, insert your A and R scores below. (Refer back to the A & R Inventory.)

A Score _____   R Score _____

Analyzing Your Score

Any score—A or R—over 65 is considered high; that is, higher than the average scores of 1,000 managers who completed the A & R Inventory. Any score below 55 is considered low (lower than the average of 1,000 managers). Scores between 55 and 65 are medium, or average. Now here are the three basic patterns of A and R results:

1. *High A—Low R*

   Your energy goes into striving to influence events and people. You do not put as much of your energy into seeking out or responding to others as do most other managers.

2. *High R—Low A*

   Your energy goes into seeking out or accommodating to others. You do not pursue your interests as directly or vigorously as most other managers. You focus on the needs, goals, and resources of others.

3. *Medium A—Medium R*

   You have a relatively balanced approach; you give information and you seek information; you protect and are concerned with your rights, beliefs, and feelings and are also concerned with the rights, beliefs, and feelings of others. You use your energy both to act upon and to tune in to the environment. In some instances a balanced score may indicate either ambivalence and inconsistency or a middle-of-the-road compromising approach. You will have to do some soul searching and get feedback from others to interpret your results accurately. In addition, a second questionnaire (see Chapter 2) will help you in clarifying your patterns.

Results from 1,000 Managers

These basic modes will be broken down later into more specific patterns of behavior. First, here are the results from 1,000 managers who completed the A and R format:

1. Higher-level managers generally had balanced scores averaging between 55 and 65 in A and R. Very few higher-level managers had R scores of less than 50. Most higher-level managers had higher A scores than R scores.

2. First-level supervisors had high R scores, averaging 65 or over. As previously noted, higher-level managers had higher A scores than lower-level managers. The indication here is that successful managers are more ready to state their views and to push for results. It is important to note, however, that there are many exceptions to this generalization. For example, one successful top executive earning over $150,000 a year had an R score of 90 and an A score of 30. Thus, he saw himself and was seen by many of his associates as being more responsive than assertive. Many successful managers have high R scores, but very few have R scores of over 70.

3. A and R scores vary depending upon the organizational context. For example, in one company about 40 first- and second-level supervisors were asked to complete the A & R Inventory. The results showed that most of these first- and second-level managers saw themselves as having higher R scores than most managers at the same level in other organizations. When this phenomenon was discussed with some of the individuals involved, it became clear that they were operating in a highly controlled situation, with constraints placed on them by their own managers, by certain federal regulations, and by the traditions of the company in which they worked.

It is important to note that your A and R scores are not simply a function of your own personality and experience. They are greatly influenced by the norms and expectations of the organization in which you work. Continuing with the example used above, however, we find it interesting that upper-level managers in this same organization were seen by their subordinates as having A scores much higher than their R scores and higher than similarly placed executives in other companies. The upper-level managers scored themselves as higher in A than their subordinates. Thus it appears that in some authoritarian systems where there are tight controls and constraints imposed by the traditions of the organization, by outside pressures, or by a somewhat autocratic management, it may be necessary for lower- and middle-level managers to become more assertive in order to break through these constraints.

WHAT IS BEST?

There is no best way to interact with others. There are times when either A or R behavior is appropriate, and there are individuals who are more effective in one mode than another. Some managers are able to get things done by involving others and using a minimum of active direction. Others tend to supervise and control their subordinates and seem to check on every detail. Your leadership style is, in part, a reflection of your experience and personality, and in part emerges from the nature of the problems and the internal and organizational pressures that are acting upon you. It is inappropriate to assume that A behavior or R behavior—if either is used to the exclusion of the other most of the time—is the optimum approach to leadership. Most successful managers integrate A and R behavior. They interact with others rather than try to please everybody or dominate those around them.

COMBINING A AND R

The most serious obstacle to personal growth and leadership effectiveness is the either-or approach to behavior. The leader is *either* strong *or* he or she is weak. The leader is *either* self-serving *or* he or she is more interested in the goals of the organization than in personal success. The leader is *either* a listener *or* a talker, a driver *or* a motivator, a lover *or* a fighter, a lone-wolf *or* a team player.

The fact is that successful leadership behavior—and also personal fulfillment and satisfaction—requires acceptance of the idea that diverse and even opposite feelings, ideas, and behavior can exist in the same organization and, more importantly, within the same person at the same time.

The A & R Inventory dramatizes and illustrates the contrasting behavior which may, at first, seem contradictory but which can coexist as you work with others. *It is neither necessary nor desirable to deny one aspect of your behavior in order to maximize another.* There is nothing to indicate that the presence of a great deal of A behavior within an individual blocks the presence of an even higher degree of R behavior. Conversely, one who is more R than A in contrast to another may nevertheless use a great deal of his or her energy to shape events. Thus, you can actively compete with your peers in some areas and be responsive and cooperative in order to accomplish departmental or organizational goals. Within any human interaction you can give information *and* seek information, you can utilize your own resources *and* the resources of others, and you can be concerned with your own rights *and* with the rights of others.

Everyone uses both A and R patterns. Of the 1,000 or more persons who have completed the A & R Inventory indicating their inclination toward a particular combination of A and R actions and reactions, not one has ever scored himself or herself as a zero on either A or R behavior. Everyone uses both aspects of his or her resources. Everyone expresses his or her views, making attempts to influence others some of the time. Everyone listens to or is in some fashion influenced by others.

The way in which you combine your needs and desires to shape events and actively defend yourself with your needs and desires to respond to the environment and gain the affection of those around you merits your careful assessment.

YOU DECIDE   The A & R Inventory gives you a brief, summary look at your own predisposition as a leader. You can choose to maintain and reinforce your present patterns; you can choose to put more of your energy into initiating action, shaping events, and influencing people; you can choose to put more effort into drawing out others, developing responsiveness and increased sensitivity to your environment; you can choose to strive for an improved balance in the application of your A and R resources. In the next chapter these choices will be made more clear. You will have an opportunity to:

1. Clarify your present leadership behavior;
2. Clarify alternatives available to you and become more aware of your options and their usefulness; and
3. Decide how you want to behave.

In subsequent chapters specific patterns of A and R behavior will be identified. You will have additional opportunities to assess your own behavior and to identify and practice those patterns which you choose to develop.

NOTES   1.   ©Educational Systems and Designs, Inc., Westport, Conn., 1978. Reprinted by permission.

2.   The use of "rights" as a component in analyzing interaction patterns was introduced by Emmons and Alberti. See R. E. Alberti and M. E. Emmons, *Your Perfect Right: A Guide to Assertive Behavior*, San Luis Obispo, Calif. (Box 1094), 1970. Wolpe and Lazarus first introduced the idea of associating "rights" with assertiveness in *Behavior Therapy Techniques* (Wolpe, J., and Lazarus, A.A., New York, Pergamon Press, 1966—now out of print), and the role of rights in interpersonal affairs became a much more popular consideration as a result of the book *Your Perfect Right*.

2

A Leadership Model

THE LEADERSHIP PROCESS

The leadership process always involves interactions between you and others. Your leadership behavior is always comprised of a combination of the A and R modes. At times you influence others, at times you are influenced by them. At times you focus on your goals, your interests, your ideas; at times you respond to or seek out the goals, interests, or ideas of others; at times you integrate your goals and needs with the goals and needs of others. In any case, your approach to leadership takes on increasingly specific form as you move into specific situations. The Leadership Profile which follows will aid you in analyzing your present patterns of behavior.

LEADERSHIP PROFILE. INTRODUCTION

The A & R Inventory gave you an overview of your leadership orientation. The Leadership Profile breaks down A and R behavior into specific patterns. The chances are that as you look over the profile questionnaire that follows you can decide which answers are right and pick those answers in arriving at your own score. The profile has been designed for your own use to aid you in analyzing the way in which you deal with problems and people and to provide a basis for further experimentation and study. You are asked to complete the questionnaire, treating each question as realistically as possible. Try to think of specific situations that you have experienced that are relevant to the question, then answer from your perception of your own behavior in these situations. Here is a hypothetical example to demonstrate how the questionnaire works.

HYPOTHETICAL SITUATION

Assume you are driving through a small suburban town, staying within the speed limit, and there are people crossing the street from time to time. Children are at play, and conditions are those that one generally finds in a small suburban area. You slow down as you cross an intersection. You have the right of way, but a driver traveling at high speed moves toward you and, even as you jam on your brakes, strikes your car and badly crumples the front end. The driver gets out of his/her car and approaches you. Below you will find four alternative responses that you might make in this situation. Rank those patterns; place a 1 in the box opposite the behavior that would, in your opinion, be most typical of you in this situation; that is, the action you would be most likely to take. Put a 4 in the box opposite the behavior that would be least likely for you, and continue ranking the remaining two statements to represent the other most likely choices. The choices are as follows:

RANK

A₂   A₁   R₁   R₂

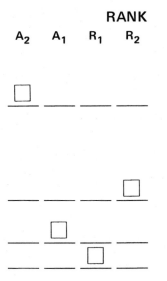

a) You storm out of the car and find yourself saying some nasty things to the individual who just side-swiped you. You know you are putting him/her down and you just go ahead and do it.

b) You are upset but you realize these things happen, that the person did not do it on purpose, and that perhaps you were a little careless yourself. You find yourself saying something like: "I am sorry I couldn't stop more quickly. You were going pretty fast but I know how these things happen. Sorry if I helped to cause the problem."

c) You say something like: "I think you were driving too fast. This is a suburban area and I am disturbed by the way you drove here in town."

d) You say: "Are you hurt? What happened?"

You may know that it is not desirable or appropriate to put other people down, but you may find that the first alternative, (a), is the most descriptive of your own behavior in this kind of a situation. If so, you should have placed a 1 in the box to the left of (a). On the other hand, you may know from your own past experience that in situations like this you tend to take blame and become apologetic. In that case you should have placed a 1 in the box to the left of alternative (b). The goal in ranking these choices is to come as close as possible to describing your actual behavior. Therefore, don't answer by selecting what you think is "best" but rank the responses in the order of how you have actually behaved when faced with situations like this in the past. The balance of the situations, which will be the basis of the self-test, are management and business oriented. You will note that the boxes which contain your rankings fall into columns designated A₂, A₁, R₁, and R₂. These designations will be used later.

INSTRUCTIONS You will find four situations described on the following pages. In each situation four alternative responses are shown. Thus for Situation 1 you will find alternatives (a), (b), (c), and (d); for Situation 2 you will find new alternatives, (a), (b), (c), and (d) relevant to that situation. Situations 3 and 4 will also each have four alternatives. First read Situation 1 and the four alternatives. Select the alternative that comes closest to describing how you would actually behave or you feel you might behave in responding to the situation. Note that to the left of the alternatives there are columns and boxes for inserting your answers. Place a 1 in the box to the left of the alternative you have chosen as coming closest to your own behavior. Now choose the alternative that is *least* descriptive of how you would behave in this situation and rank it 4. Place a 4 in the box to the left of the statement you have chosen. Then rank the remaining statements 2 and 3. Place the 2 and 3 in the boxes in the columns to your left. The four codings A_2, A_1, R_1, and R_2 at the top of the columns will be used later to aid you in totaling your score and in interpreting your results. When you have completed the profile you will obtain your total score by adding the numbers in each column. Details for scoring and interpretation will be provided at the end of the profile.

SITUATION 1

You have a subordinate (or someone assigned to you) working for you who is not performing in accordance with expectations and goals that you and she/he have discussed on quite a few occasions. Assume as part of normal operating practice that you once again are about to review this individual's performance. Pick and number with 1 the statement below which is most representative of how you might respond, after an introductory statement has been made by you such as, "I asked you in today to review your performance." Rank the following statements 1 through 4.

RANK

A$_2$ A$_1$ R$_1$ R$_2$

a) Tell me how you feel things have been going and what you would like to see happening in the future.

b) We have talked several times about your work goals and your results are not up to the level we agreed upon. I want you to improve your performance.

c) It looks to me like you are just careless and irresponsible, or maybe you just don't have what it takes to do this job.

d) You know it is my job to bring you in every once in a while and talk over how things are going. I hope this does not upset you and I want to be as fair and helpful as I can. I don't see any reason why we can't have a friendly talk and review how things have been going. Certainly, if there is anything I can do to help you, I want to do it.

SITUATION 2

The boss calls you into the office and criticizes you for being over the budget. You have spent more money than you anticipated this month on certain supplies that were essential because of an increased workload and some changes in demand from the people to whom you provide services. The boss is not only critical, but puts you down and accuses you of careless management. Which of the following responses would be most typical of you when unjustly criticized by someone in higher authority? Rank the following statements 1 through 4.

RANK

A_2 A_1 R_1 R_2

a) I am sorry you are dissatisfied with my results. I have been trying very hard to live up to your expectations. I would appreciate any help you can give me.

b) Every dollar I spent was to meet the needs of the groups that I service. If you know of a better way to do things, you should have told me.

c) I can see you are dissatisfied. Could you give me some specific information as to how you see the issue of cost-effectiveness on this project?

d) It is true that we spent more money this month than we budgeted. There was a greatly increased demand for our services. I can demonstrate that these expenditures were necessary and cost-effective.

SITUATION 3

Another group, or department, requests extra materials or services from you. You have been having a lot of trouble meeting your goals and budgets and would prefer not to make these extra services or materials available. Rank the following statements 1 through 4.

RANK

A_2 A_1 R_1 R_2

a) I cannot provide these extra services right now. We are way behind and I must use every resource I have to get this department's work out.

b) You have some nerve asking me for help when you know I am snowed under.

c) I am really up against the wall. It would be very difficult for me to help you at this time. I do want you to know that I am concerned about your situation and I want to do everything I can. Maybe I can provide a little help. Please try to understand that it will be tough for me if I give you very much.

d) Tell me a little more about the problem and let's explore some of the ways we might approach it.

SITUATION 4

A top executive asks you to increase the amount of effort you're putting into a given project (Project X). In your opinion, it would be a mistake to increase emphasis on this project. You recognize the person involved has a great deal of experience, knowledge, and authority. You have been quite close to this issue and you feel strongly that it should be de-emphasized. Rank the following statements 1 through 4.

RANK

A_2 A_1 R_1 R_2

a) If you want us to move ahead on this, you have my support and I will do whatever I can to make it come out the way you want. I do have a few reservations about it, but in view of your experience and background I must go the way you suggest.

b) It is possible to do it the way you want. You have been awfully busy upstairs with some problems and have not had much time to stay close to this one. You are not really as well informed as you think. If you give it a little more time and analyze it fully, you will have to reconsider your position.

c) I understand that you want a change in emphasis on Project X. I would like to know more about what your expectations would be as a result of the change.

d) Project X is cost-effective. If we put more emphasis on it, we will increase our costs without much payout. There are several other activities that are inefficient. I would like to clean up those projects and make the whole operation more profitable.

SCORING YOUR PROFILE

By ranking the alternatives for each of the four situations, you have indicated patterns of behavior that you utilize in dealing with management situations. These patterns have been designated as A_2, A_1, R_1, and R_2. Each pattern will be described later as you interpret your profile results. The first step in getting ready to utilize these results is to obtain totals for all four of the situations. This is accomplished by adding the numbers in each column. The specific steps for scoring follow.

Add all of the numbers in the first column following each of the four situations. Thus, go back to Situation 1 and read down the first column designated A_2 until you come to the box in that column. The number in that box is your score on the A_2 column for Situation 1. Do the same for Situations 2, 3, and 4. Add the numbers from the box in the first column, A_2, for Situations 1, 2, 3, and 4 to arrive at your A_2 total, that is, the total of all your rankings in column A_2. Insert your total in the profile summary score shown below. Now repeat the process for column A_1, that is, add the number for each of the four situations as they appear in the second column, A_1. Insert your total under A_1 in the profile summary score shown below. Do the same for columns R_1 and R_2. Enter your totals below.

Profile Summary Score

A_2	A_1	R_1	R_2

These totals will be used to aid you in interpreting your Leadership Profile. First each of the four patterns A_2, A_1, R_1, and R_2 will be described.

CLARIFYING YOUR LEADERSHIP PATTERN

In order to interpret the meaning of your scores, you need precise definitions of the terms used to describe your leadership behavior. Words like Aggressive and Responsive will be used, not as they are defined in the dictionary, but as they relate specifically to the A and R leadership patterns discussed previously.

A Patterns

All A behavior focuses on your goals, your rights, and your resources. When you are behaving in the A mode you express your views, you do not permit yourself to be pushed around, and you value and defend your own rights and feelings. There is, however, a significant difference between A_2 and A_1, behavior. A_1 behavior is Assertive. A_2 behavior is Aggressive. When you are behaving *assertively* (A_1), you pursue your goals, use your resources to influence people and events, and stand up for your rights without violating the rights, denying or exploiting the resources, or stifling the individuality of others. When you pursue your goals, influence people, and stand up for your rights in a way that violates the rights of others, exploits them, or denies their individuality and the value of their resources, you are behaving *aggressively* (A_2).

In more popular terms, Assertive and Aggressive behavior both involve going after what you want and not permitting others to push you around. The key difference between these behaviors is in *how* you define and pursue your goals and how you defend yourself. Again, in popular terms, if in the process of pursuing your goals, you adopt a win-lose attitude, if you put people down, you are being Aggressive. If you go after what you want and defend yourself without putting people down you are being Assertive.

R Patterns Like the A pattern, the R patterns have basic similarities. All R behavior focuses on "the other"—what does the other want, how does the other feel, how do you choose to react to the resources and rights of the other. There are two basic patterns for acting on your R concerns; the Responsive pattern and the Nonassertive pattern. There are significant differences between Responsive behavior (R_1) and Nonassertive behavior (R_2).

When you seek out, react to, and show concern for the needs, goals, rights, and resources of others without denying your own rights, resources, needs, or goals, you are being *Responsive* (R_1). When, in your efforts to react to, show concern for, and respect the rights and resources of others, you deny your own rights, resources, needs or goals, or fail to defend yourself, you are being *Nonassertive* (R_2).

Once again, in popular terms, if you permit yourself to be put down without standing up for yourself, you are behaving nonassertively. Listening, asking questions, showing concern for the rights of others, are patterns of behavior which are useful and appropriate; they are not denials of your individuality, rights, or resources; they are, therefore, Responsive patterns.

In later chapters the nature and appropriateness of various A and R patterns of behavior will be described.

INTERPRETING YOUR PROFILE First insert the totals from the Profile Summary Score.

Since you placed a 1 next to the statements you felt were most descriptive of your behavior, the result is that *the lower the score, the more you feel the statement was descriptive of your behavior.* So if you chose A_2 items as number 1 for each situation, this would mean the A_2 responses would total 4 (4 items rated 1 = 4). Conversely, if you rejected the A_2 statement each time it appeared, if you gave it a 4, your total would be 16 (4 items rated 4 = 16).

Understanding Your Profile

Each pattern (each column) represents variations of A behavior or R behavior as have been discussed:

A_2 = Aggressive behavior
A_1 = Assertive behavior
R_1 = Responsive behavior
R_2 = Nonassertive (relinquishing) behavior

Your profile should be read as follows:

1. First, the lowest number in the profile shows the specific pattern you find most descriptive of your behavior; (for example, a low score in R_1 indicates that you see yourself as Responsive).

2. The highest number in the profile shows the pattern least descriptive of you (for example, a high score in R_2 means you see yourself as rarely Nonassertive).

3. The remaining patterns will fall into second and third place.

4. When two or more columns have similar totals—A_1 (Assertive) might be 5 and R_1 (Responsive) might be 5—this indicates that you see yourself as using both modes almost interchangeably, or in combination with each other.

THE LEADERSHIP MODEL. A SUMMARY

The four basic patterns of behavior can be illustrated by the use of a graphic model. The model is built step by step to aid you in identifying and clarifying basic modes of leadership behavior.

First, there are two basic patterns of behavior which are always present, as leaders and other organization members interact to set goals, solve problems, and deal with conflict. These patterns describe *what* you do as you act and react in leadership situations.

A Pattern: What you do	*R Pattern: What you do*
Go after what you want—shape events.	Seek out the feelings and views of others.
Express yourself.	Tune into the environment.
Defend yourself.	Express concern for the rights and feelings of others.

Within each of these two patterns which describe your options in terms of *what* you choose to do, there are two subpatterns which describe *how* you do it.

A Pattern   A₁   You can follow the A pattern without putting others down. This is Assertive behavior.

A₂   You can follow the A pattern and in the process put others down. This is Aggressive behavior.

R Pattern   R₁   You can follow the R pattern without denying your own rights or resources, without putting yourself down. This is Responsive behavior.

R₂   You can follow the R pattern in ways which deny your own rights and resources, that is, you can put yourself down. This is Nonassertive behavior.

These patterns can now be pictured as a circle representing the full range of actions and reactions available to you as you interact with others (Fig. 1).

Note that all behavior to the left of the perpendicular line is active, aimed at influencing others and defending yourself. All behavior to the right of the line is reactive, aimed at seeking out, understanding, fitting in with, or responding to the influence and rights of others.

All behavior below the horizontal line violates other's rights or permits them to violate yours; it involves putdowns of yourself or others. All behavior above the line shows a concern and respect for the rights and resources of both parties.

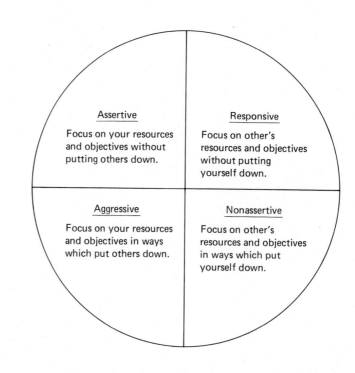

Fig. 1. The Leadership Model. (Source: © Educational Systems and Designs, Inc., Westport, Conn., 1978. Reprinted by permission.)

Assertive and Responsive behavior are, in effect, opposite sides of the same coin. They are open, interactive, problem-solving modes. They can be integrated. In contrast, Aggressive and Nonassertive behavior tend to push people away from interaction. Aggressive behavior demonstrates a preoccupation with winning, with being one-up. Nonassertive behavior manifests a need to be liked, to fit in, to avoid interaction or confrontation. Thus, Aggressive and Nonassertive behavior cannot be integrated—they may occur in the same person or they may stem from similar sources: self-doubt, defensiveness, or low self-esteem. However, Aggressive behavior moves out without adequate concern for others, while Nonassertiveness turns in without adequate concern for self. In brief terms, the following statements quickly demonstrate why Assertive and Responsive behavior are interactive and can be integrated, and Aggressive and Nonassertive behavior are divergent and isolate one from others.

Assertive: What I feel and believe is important.
Responsive: What you feel and believe is important.
Aggressive: What I feel and believe is important; what you feel and believe is not.
Nonassertive: What you feel and believe is important; what I feel and believe is not.

It is emotionally possible and intellectually valid to value your own ideas and value the ideas of others. It makes sense to combine Assertiveness and Responsiveness. It is emotionally and intellectually *im*possible to combine simultaneously the feeling: "My ideas are valuable, I do not care about yours" (Aggressive) with the feeling: "My ideas are not important, I care about yours" (Nonassertive). You cannot value yourself and others while simultaneously putting others down or permitting them to put you down.

CONCLUSION Although every individual is unique and functions in a unique environment, there are basic patterns of behavior that are always present in leadership situations. The Leadership Model defines four basic patterns which all organization members use at one time or another. Everyone has, on occasion, been Aggressive or Nonassertive. Everyone has been Assertive or Responsive. The Model sets forth these four options. The next issue is how you utilize your resources, how you act as you pursue your objectives and relate to others. Are you Aggressive, Responsive, Assertive, or Nonassertive? Do you really know how you come across? The next chapter is designed to help you in further clarifying your present behavior and determining whether you wish to make changes in your leadership actions.

3

Where Are You? Where Do You Choose To Be?

SELF-ASSESSMENT By analyzing your response to the A & R Inventory and the Leadership Profile, and by examining the Leadership Model, you can discover some specific information about your current behavior. You may find from the A & R Inventory that you have been underutilizing either your A or your R resources. You may find from the Leadership Profile that you are more Aggressive or more Nonassertive than you realized. You may, however, find that your scores are reasonably well-balanced. Managers from hundreds of organizations have described their managerial styles and behavior as Assertive and/or Responsive in completing forms like those you have completed; and, in addition, in follow-up interviews most managers describe themselves as combining Assertive and Responsive behavior in various ways in order to achieve their goals.

It is rare for a manager to describe him/herself as Aggressive or Nonassertive. The fact is that the very people who see themselves as Assertive or Responsive are seen by others—at least part of the time—as Aggressive or Nonassertive. The A & R Inventory and the Leadership Profile scores give you an indication of your own self-image. It is important to give consideration to the fact that there may be a significant gap between how you see yourself and how others see you.

How Do You Really Come Across? Given the fact that you can rationalize your behavior and can kid yourself, and given the fact that interviews and training programs involving thousands of managers show there is almost always a gap between how they think they are behaving and how they are seen by others, it follows that objective self-assessment is a challenging process. In order to obtain an accurate picture of your impact on others, it is essential, in one way or another, to get feedback. How does your husband or wife see you? How do your boss, associates, and subordinates see you? How do you come across when you're under pressure, when you feel you are being attacked? The answers to these questions require a manifest desire to listen, a willingness to seek out the views of others, and the skill to create more candid communications. You have some specific alternatives available to you:

1. You can ask your associates, subordinates, or your boss how they see you in regard to managerial actions and problem-solving endeavors. Are you seen as Assertive—giving information, expressing goals, persuading, controlling, without soliciting the views of others? Are you Responsive—listening, probing, responding, without initiating action or letting others know how you feel? Are you combining Assertiveness and Responsiveness in an effective, interactive style?

2. You can review your own profiles and examine your own behavior more carefully, thinking through ways in which you respond in difficult and tense situations.

3. You can administer the same kinds of formats that you completed yourself to your boss, associates, or subordinates, asking them to complete the formats based on how they see you (see Appendix A).

4. Finally, you can become more aware of the verbal and nonverbal cues and clues that people are giving you. People have ways of letting you know how you are coming across without actually and overtly telling you. They send out a variety of messages. You can clarify your own leadership behavior and impact by tuning in to these messages. The checklists below will aid you in assessing how you have been coming across to others.

Checklist 1. Are You Aggressive?

If and when you are Aggressive, people may react in one or more of the following ways:

_____ People at times draw away from you or fail to make eye contact. They seem edgy or nervous.

_____ People at times seem to have a chip on their shoulder, more so in dealing with you than in dealing with others.

_____ When dealing with you, people sometimes become careful, tentative, and guarded.

_____ People rarely disagree with you and avoid crossing you.

_____ People do not bring their problems or questions to you.

_____ People may try to "get" you (put you down or embarrass you) with humor or subtle contempt.

_____ Those above you often give you the tough jobs in dealing with people because you have a thick skin.

Checklist 2. Are You Nonassertive?

If and when you are nonassertive, others may react as follows:

_____ They may try too hard to reassure you, to make you feel O. K.

_____ They may move in and dominate you (because they feel you won't stand up for your rights).

_____ They may tend to dismiss your ideas, fail to seek out your opinions.

_____ They may try to avoid you (they don't want to feel guilty or uncomfortable as a result of your apologetic or self-pitying behavior).

_____ They may lack animation or excitement when dealing with you.

_____ They may fail to challenge, push, or involve you.

_____ They may rarely ask you to take on the tough tasks in dealing with people. You are too easy-going.

_____ They may become condescending or patronizing (they are afraid to attack you directly because they feel you can't take it).

Interpreting the Checklists

Clearly, these and similar signals may be the result of the other person's self-doubt, strong need to win, or unwillingness to be straightforward. However, by tuning in to these reactions and observing how these same people treat others, you can determine whether they are reacting to you or acting out some of their own needs and problems.

If you are being Assertive and Responsive, there is a good chance that people will come to you with their problems, confront you when they disagree, listen to your ideas, make eye contact with you, and involve you in tasks which require strength and flexibility.

Research and Personal Choice

As you engage in an examination of your own behavior, you may choose to strive to become more Assertive and Responsive; you may choose to reduce your Aggressive or Nonassertive behavior. On the other hand, you may feel that you can be more effective by being more Aggressive or by being accommodating to others. Before pursuing specific behavioral goals it is useful to review the highlights of the research and observations of those who have studied managerial behavior.

THE ORGANIZATION AND THE LEADER

The overriding conclusion of dozens of research efforts regarding leadership effectiveness is that Assertive and Responsive behaviors, combined in various ways, produce better results than Aggressive or Nonassertive behaviors. Most of these behavioral studies have been organization-oriented; they have attempted to determine which patterns of leadership and organizational behavior contribute to the achievement of organizational goals such as productivity, profits, morale, and institutional growth. The results of these efforts are dramatically similar:

1. Leaders who strive to attain organizational purpose and show concern for the needs and interests of others get better results than those who ignore or deprecate others or those who fail to acknowledge or act on their own achievements or power drives.[1]
2. Leaders who are preoccupied with being liked, who are more concerned with affiliation than with results, are less effective than their more self-possessed, task-oriented counterparts.[2]
3. Participatory methods which reflect a genuine concern for the rights, needs, goals, and resources of others have, over and over again, been shown to produce positive results.[3]
4. Leaders who are authoritarian, autocratic, and unresponsive to others are less effective than those who are straightforward and available to others.[4]

The terminology used in describing leadership behavior in these studies varies, but the basic meaning of what is being said is generally consistent with the styles and patterns described in the Leadership Model.

For example, Blake and Mouton,[5] in identifying managers who were successful leaders, describe them as willing to confront conflict, task-oriented *and* concerned with people, and usually able to change their minds when faced with new evidence. McClelland[6] describes the successful leaders identified in his studies as both motivated by power drives *and* willing and able to socialize and inhibit their power drives so as not to exploit, demean, or ignore others. In the language of the Leadership Model, both Blake's and McClelland's successful leaders are Assertive—they pursue goals, are active and affirmative. They are also Responsive—they recognize and react to the forces present in the environment. In the Texas Instruments and General Electric Studies,[7] successful managers were described as being respected and responded to by their subordinates because they let people know where they stood, and interacted with their subordinates rather than dominating or coddling them. Over and over again the researchers and observers point out that win-lose and punitive, authoritarian behavior are not optimum, that aggression as a major managerial mode doesn't pay. Similarly, affiliation-oriented, soft, relinquishing styles of leadership do not produce results; Nonassertive or other-oriented behavior is not the answer. *There is not one study in the annals of organizational research which shows that win-lose (Aggressive) behavior or behavior which manifests a preoccupation with being liked (Nonassertive) is effective over the long run.*

THE NEW PERSPECTIVE

Many researchers and observers of organizational behavior have focused on the needs and goals of the organization. In recent years there has been a growing concern with the needs and goals of the individual. Reisman's *The Lonely Crowd*[8] and Whyte's *The Organization Man*[9] dramatized the negative impact of the *organization* and the growing alienation of the individual from the organization and the larger society. Whereas from 1930 to 1950 the focus of organizational improvement vacillated between making individuals better organization members versus making organizations more humane and hospitable to individuals, attention in the 1960s and 1970s has shifted toward the individual's needs, rights, and self-interest. The concern is no longer directed solely at making the individual a *better* organization member or changing the norms and patterns of the organization so it will be more supportive to people, although both concerns are still present. The emphasis is now on the individual and how he or she controls and develops his or her own resources and takes responsibility for his or her own behavior.

Books like *Your Perfect Right,*[10] *Creative Aggression,*[11] *I'm OK—You're OK,*[12] *How to Be Your Own Best Friend,*[13] *Born to Win,*[14] *Don't Say Yes When You Want to Say No,*[15] *Your Erroneous Zones,*[16] have sold in the millions. These popular and prescriptive approaches to self-enhancement and fulfillment are rooted in more rigorous and scholarly work which has placed increasing emphasis on the autonomy of the individual and his or her capacity to utilize a wider range of resources and take charge of his/her life. Gestalt psychology[17] and in-depth application of assertiveness training[18] have been major sources of these efforts. A common thread running through these and dozens of other self-help books, courses, and in-depth studies is that *you* have the capacity and the right to pursue your own goals, to value and utilize your own resources, and to stand up for yourself. Your feelings, your concerns, your needs are worthy of your attention. Although the totality of you is you interacting with others, in the best sense you come first. It is only through valuing and defending yourself that you can feel good about yourself and it is essential to feel good about yourself if you are to feel good about others. The new perspective is that effective interactions start with you, with your getting in touch with your own resources and defining your own goals.

THE FUTURE: WHERE YOU WANT TO BE

For the first time in the history of management and organizational development there is now a confluence of ideas and values which make it possible to fuse personal growth and organizational improvement. Clearly, your ability to lead in ways that research and experience suggest are most effective requires you to act and react, to assert yourself, and to respond to others. If interactive, open, participatory methods are organizationally valid—as both research and the preferences of thousands of managers indicate—then developing the capacity to value and act upon your own beliefs and resources *and* to value and react to beliefs and resources of others is integral to improved organizational effectiveness. More importantly, at least in the eyes of many, standing up for *yourself*, pursuing what *you* want while being aware of and concerned with the people around you is the key to personal fulfillment and emotional health.

SUMMARY

Research, self-assessment, the personal preferences expressed by large numbers of managers,[19] and recently emerging concerns with the personal rights and personal growth of individuals all support the value of Assertive and Responsive behavior. Even with the generalizations, formulas, and "ideal" patterns of behavior described in research and supported by personal experience, there is still ample room for the uniqueness of the individual. Your personality is different from everyone else's. The content of what you say, your tone of voice, your gestures, your facial expressions are different from all others. The ways in which you deal with your own and others' anger, impatience, affection, and anxiety, and face the many emotions that are present in human interactions together determine the nature of the interactions between you, a unique individual, and the environment, or the people around you. Your environment is different from all other environments. Your boss, your subordinates, the problems you face are different from the boss's, subordinates', and problems experienced by others. Given all these variables— your individuality, your unique environment, and the changing problems you face—it follows that your leadership patterns are unlike the patterns of others. The one inescapable requirement for change and improvement is the belief that drawing upon your individuality, your values, your environment, you have the right and the capacity to make choices regarding leadership actions. You make the choices; you are responsible for, and in control of, your own behavior. A Planning and Development Guide is appended to this chapter. By reviewing the formats provided, you can pin down your own behavior and leadership goals. Your choices, your actions will be greatly influenced by what you know—this chapter has dealt with information that has been aimed at clarifying the advantages of Assertive and Responsive behavior. The second critical ingredient in determining your behavior is what you feel. The chapter that follows deals with your most important leadership resources—your emotions, your drives and feelings, and how they can influence your actions. In each succeeding chapter, attention will be paid to "how to": how to get in touch with your resources and apply them effectively. Before proceeding to the next chapter, complete the Planning and Development Guide which follows.

PLANNING AND DEVELOPMENT GUIDE

INTRODUCTION   As you assess your communication and leadership behavior it is useful to link that behavior with your personal goals and intentions. Several formats have been provided to aid you in thinking through where you want to be. The first of these formats deals with job factors and is designed to aid you in clarifying some of your on-the-job objectives and interests. The next format asks you to identify your own resources, satisfactions, and skills. The remaining formats are designed to assist you in specifying behavioral objectives and relating them to Assertive-Responsive behavior.

FORMAT I. WHAT DO I WANT[20]

This form is designed to help you identify some of the broad areas in which you would like change to occur. Review each item and then check Column 1, 2, or 3.

	I choose to change significantly. 1	I choose to change somewhat. 2	I choose to stay about the same. 3
1. Earnings ($'s)			
2. Recognition			
3. Personal satisfaction			
4. Tasks or assignments			
5. The basic nature of the work (includes possibility of changing jobs or careers)			
6. How I am seen by others (associates, managers, other workers, or professionals)			
7. Personal effectiveness			
8. Other			
9. Other			

FORMAT II. WHAT HAVE I GOT?

JOB RELATED RESOURCES AND SATISFACTIONS

1. List: What do I do well? (Indicate functions, activities, skills that you perform well.)

_____

_____

_____

_____

_____

_____

2. List: What do I enjoy doing? (Indicate job activities that give you most satisfaction.)

_____

_____

_____

_____

_____

_____

3. List: What are my resources? (Indicate talents, traits, capacities, such as intelligence, sense of humor, ambition, etc.)

_____

_____

_____

_____

_____

_____

FORMAT III. BEHAVIORAL GOALS

INTRODUCTION   The questionnaires and formats that have been provided earlier have been aimed at aiding you in analyzing your own communication and leadership patterns. You are now asked to (1) summarize those patterns, (2) analyze your strengths, and (3) set behavioral goals and objectives for yourself. Consider ways in which you are presently using your resources and ways in which you connect with, and get satisfaction from, what you do.

YOUR PRESENT PATTERN

Based on everything you know about yourself and everything you have learned in thinking through your present modes of behavior, summarize your behavior in the format provided below.

a) Are you Aggressive?

1. ___ Sometimes I step on people's toes or rub people the wrong way.

2. ___ Sometimes I express my anger by attacking others.

3. ___ I know that I am more impatient and pushy than is appropriate.

4. ___ I find myself acting resentful and vindictive more often than I would like.

5. ___ I have been told that I am too aggressive and I should try to be less abrasive.

6. ___ I recognize that I am sometimes carried away by my desire to win, to prevail, to be in control.

Comments: Do you want to change? What? How?

_____

_____

_____

_____

_____

_____

b) Are you Nonassertive?

1. ___ Sometimes I back down pretty easily.

2. ___ I try too hard to please people and to keep everybody happy.

3. ___ I become quite tense and nervous when I have to deal with conflict or unpleasant situations.

4. ___ I find it hard to be direct; I tend to try to take a soft approach and avoid confrontations.

5. ___ I have been told by others that I should be more firm and should express myself more directly.

6. ____ There are quite a few times when, after a situation is over, I feel I should have acted more firmly in my own best interest.

Comments: Do you want to change? What? How?

_____

_____

_____

_____

_____

_____

c) Are you Assertive?

1. ____ I have little difficulty in expressing myself succinctly, clearly, and straightforwardly.

2. ____ I can deal with conflict and disagreement without becoming overly tense and angry or backing off and compromising inappropriately.

3. ____ I have no trouble letting people know where they stand; I am able to give the information without alienating them or "copping out."

4. ____ I am effectively using my A resources (my drive, creativity, capacity to pursue goals, and ability to defend myself).

5. ____ I feel good about myself and able to go after what I want.

6. ____ Other people, in general, are responsive to my ideas.

Comments: Do you want to change? What? How?

_____

_____

_____

_____

_____

_____

d) Are you Responsive?

1. ____ I am able to draw out other people, listen, and respond without compromising my own position.

2. ____ I have an interest in and capacity to relate to the changing environment and the people in it.

3. ____ I have no trouble asking questions, modifying my own position when it is appropriate, and generally being open and available to other people.

4. ____ I am able to use my R resources effectively (my concern and empathy for others, my desire to be cooperative and work effectively in teams or groups).

5. ____ I have no trouble in accepting compliments or affection from others.

6. ____ I have no trouble in showing other people that I am concerned and care about them.

Comments: Do you want to change? What? How?

_____

_____

_____

_____

_____

_____

FORMAT IV. DO YOU WANT TO CHANGE?

In using these brief checklists and analyses of your present patterns and strengths, you have been asked: "Do you want to change?" Do you want to become less Aggressive, more Assertive, more Responsive, less Nonassertive? Do you want to pursue your goals more affirmatively? Do you want to increase your ability to draw out and build upon the resources of others? Are there ways in which you can use your own talents more effectively? As you think through these questions you can become more specific about the steps you need to take to get where you want to go. For example, if you want more recognition, if you want to increase your earnings, if you want to have a more positive impact on people, these general objectives need to be converted into specific actions. And so the format which follows is designed to aid you in identifying action steps you wish to take and situations you want to work on in order to get from where you are to where you want to be. Specify the action steps you wish to take in order to achieve your personal, organizational, and behavioral goals.

a) Dealing with your boss. Check any of the statements below that apply.

1. ____ I choose to confront my boss about some of the criticisms, demands, or feedback he/she has given me. I want to discuss these issues specifically and resolve differences that exist between us. (Assertive)

2. ____ I choose to get more feedback from the boss regarding my own performance. (Responsive)

3. ____ I choose to establish clear-cut goals and expectations with him/her. (Assertive-Responsive)

4. ____ I choose to increase my ability to draw out the boss, to get his/her expectations, feelings, and goals regarding my operation. (Responsive)

5. ____ I choose to become more skillful in defending myself and in resolving conflict with the boss. (Assertive-Responsive)

b) Dealing with peers and subordinates.

1. ____ I choose to give those I work with a more direct indication of my expectations and goals. (Assertive)

2. ____ I choose to improve my ability to build cooperative relationships with the people with whom I work. (Responsive)

3. ____ I choose to confront obstacles, performance problems, and other areas that I have tended to let pass. (Assertive)

4. ____ I choose to come across with the people I work with as more direct, firm, and clear. (Assertive)

5. ____ I choose to conduct meetings and small-group activities in a more affirmative style without becoming dominant or abrasive. (Assertive)

6. ____ I choose to conduct meetings utilizing the resources of others, drawing others out, and involving them more effectively. (Responsive)

7. ____ I choose to become more effective at integrating my resources with the resources of others. (Assertive-Responsive)

8. ____ I choose to improve my capacity to review performance and to obtain the commitment and goal-oriented energies of others. (Assertive-Responsive)

FORMAT V. SUMMARY: WHERE DO I CHOOSE TO BE?

CHECK AND ELABORATE   Use the previous checklist (Format IV) as a basis for identifying your behavioral goals.

_____ I choose to be more Assertive.

Summary comments._____

_____

_____

_____

_____

_____ I choose to be more Responsive.

Summary comments._____

_____

_____

_____

_____

_____ I choose to be more Assertive-Responsive: to integrate my resources with the resources of others and to interact more effectively.

Summary comments._____

_____

_____

_____

_____

_____ I want to use my resources more fully.

Summary comments._____

_____

_____

_____

_____

FORMAT VI. "HOW TO" GET WHERE YOU WANT TO GO

The format which follows is designed for you to summarize your most important objectives and to describe how you choose to accomplish them. In the "How" section, identify specific behavior you feel is appropriate.

For your own clarity, draw a line after each goal. Note the following as an example:

What I Want	*How I plan to get it*
More impact on key decisions	By being more forceful at meetings. (Assertive)
	By expressing myself more often and more straightforwardly. (Assertive)
More money	By setting improvement goals and working them through with my boss. (Assertive-Responsive)

FORMAT VI

What do I want?	How do I choose to behave in order to get it?

SUMMARY In the chapters that follow, each of a wide range of action strategies will be reviewed. First, specific behaviors associated with each of the basic leadership patterns will be identified. Techniques for becoming more Assertive and Responsive will be outlined and specific procedures or models for setting objectives, reviewing performance, and confronting conflict will be defined. Methods for sharpening your skills and practicing Assertive and Responsive behavior are also described.

So from here on you are urged to consider three important self-improvement approaches.

1. Clarify your understanding of the options that are available to you; that is, the nature of and differences among Assertive, Responsive, Aggressive, and Nonassertive patterns of behavior.

2. Clarify and become closer to your own resources and feelings; learn how your emotions can be converted into constructive action.

3. Apply Assertive-Responsive techniques to general objectives and to specific goals and problems.

NOTES
1. David C. McClelland and David H. Burnham, "Power is the great motivator," *Harvard Business Review* 54, No. 2 (March-April, 1976): 100–110.

2. *Ibid.* See also David C. McClelland, *Power—The Inner Experience*, New York: John Wiley, 1975.

3. The influence of participatory methods was first documented in early work done by Lewin, Lippitt, and White. Their initial work was with children. See R. Lippitt and R. K. White, "The Social climate of children's groups," in R. G. Barker, J. Kounin, and H. Wright (Eds.), *Child Behavior and Development*, New York: McGraw-Hill, 1953, 485–508. See also K. Lewin, R. Lippitt, and R. K. White, "Patterns of aggressive behavior in experimentally created 'social climates'." *Journal of Social Psychology*, X (1939): 271–299. Later studies regarding participation in management include work by Leavitt and Bavelas. See H. J. Leavitt, "Some effects of certain communication patterns on group performance," *Journal of Abnormal and Social Psychology*, 46 (1951): 327–336; and A. Bavelas, "Communication patterns in task-oriented groups," *Journal of the Acoustical Society of America*, 22 (1950): 725–730. See also R. Likert, *New Patterns of Management*, New York: McGraw-Hill, 1961.

4. McClelland did a great deal of study regarding the impact of authoritarian behavior on managerial effectiveness. See David C. McClelland, *Power—The Inner Experience*, New York: John Wiley, 1975. A more general discussion of autocratic versus more responsive modes of behavior can be found in D. McGregor, *The Human Side of Enterprise*, New York: McGraw-Hill, 1960.

5. Robert R. Blake and Jane S. Mouton, *The Managerial Grid*, Houston: Gulf Publishing Company, 1964.

6. David C. McClelland and David H. Burnham, "Power is the great motivator," *Harvard Business Review*, 54, No. 2 (March-April, 1976): 100-110.

7. The General Electric Study can be found in Hugh Estes, "The achievement of management goals through the use of behavioral science techniques," *Engineering of Human Behavior in Industry*, Reprint Series No. 167, Ithaca, New York: Cornell University, New York State School of Industrial and Labor Relations, December, 1964. The Texas Instruments Study can be found in "Conditions for manager motivation," *Harvard Business Review*, 44, No. 1 (January-February, 1966): 58-71.

8. D. Reisman, *The Lonely Crowd*, New Haven: Yale University, 1961.

9. W. H. Whyte, Jr., *The Organization Man*, New York: Simon & Schuster, 1956.

10. R. E. Alberti and M. L. Emmons, *Your Perfect Right: A Guide to Assertive Behavior*, San Luis Obispo, Calif.: Impact, 1974.

11. George R. Bach and Herb Goldberg, *Creative Aggression: A Guide to Assertive Living*, New York: Avon, 1974.

12. Thomas A. Harris, M.D., *I'm OK—You're OK: A Practical Guide to Transactional Analysis*, New York: Harper & Row, 1969.

13. Mildred Newman and Bernard Berkowitz, *How to Be Your Own Best Friend*, New York: Ballantine, 1974.

14. M. James and D. Jongeward, *Born to Win: Transactional Analysis with Gestalt Experiments*, Reading, Mass.: Addison-Wesley, 1971.

15. Herbert Fensterheim and Jean Baer, *Don't Say Yes When You Want to Say No*, New York: Dell, 1975.

16. Wayne Dyer, *Your Erroneous Zones*, New York: Funk & Wagnalls, 1976.

17. Erving Polster and Miriam Polster, *Gestalt Therapy Integrated*, New York: Vintage, 1974. See also Frederick Perls, M.D., Ralph F. Hefferline, and Paul Goodman, *Gestalt Therapy*, New York: Dell, 1951. See also Joel Latner, *The Gestalt Therapy Book*, New York: Bantam Books, 1973.

18. Alberti, Robert E., *Assertiveness: Innovations, Applications, Issues*, Impact Publishers, Inc., San Luis Obispo, Calif., 1977.

19. The author, in collaboration with other members of Educational Systems and Designs, Inc., has gathered data regarding the personal preferences of managers in the selection of an appropriate managerial style. Over the last ten years, approximately 25,000 managers have completed a format call "Profile on Approaches to Communications" indicating their choices regarding four basic managerial approaches: the controlling approach that involves the use of sanctions and authoritarian modes of behavior; the relinquishing approach that is characterized by soft, accommodating behavior; the defensive approach that is comprised of

either aggressive or nonassertive behavior; and the developmental approach that is essentially a problem solving, interactive mode of leadership. Those completing the Communications Profile are given a series of problem situations and are asked to choose the most appropriate responses. *Every manager who has participated in this endeavor has chosen the developmental response as the most desirable in most situations.*

20. This Format is based on the Career Analysis Guide, © Educational Systems and Designs, 1975, designed by Malcolm E. Shaw and Elaine D. Carter. Reprinted by permission.

4

The Leadership Model.
Specific Patterns
of Behavior

THE CHOICES Four behavioral modes have been identified in the Leadership Model (repeated here).

A Behavior: Assertive A_1 and Aggressive A_2.
R Behavior: Responsive R_1 and Nonassertive R_2.

Each of the four major patterns of behavior described in the Leadership Model can be thought of as a strategy for dealing with the variety of situations that are faced in management and interpersonal affairs.

In any given interaction, the individuals involved may manifest any of the behaviors shown on the circle (Fig. 1) but over the long pull, for most people, one mode tends to be dominant. Some managers spend most of their time being Aggressive or Nonassertive. Others are more apt to be Assertive. When an individual spends most of his or her time in the Assertive mode, there is a built-in likelihood that responsiveness will also be present. As long as an individual is behaving in ways that do not deny the rights, resources, capacities, and potentialities of others, there is a good chance that his or her behavior will elicit involvement and responsiveness from others. Conversely, some managers may spend most of their time in the Responsive mode seeking information, showing concern, and generally maintaining an open, available stance. Again, however, as one seeks information, shows concern, and is Responsive toward others, it follows that there is a high likelihood that one will also behave assertively. Thus, if a manager is concerned about a subordinate's performance, he or she may seek out the subordinate's viewpoint,

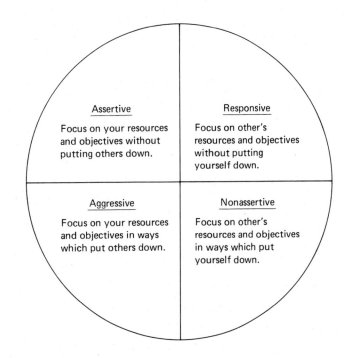

Fig. 1. The Leadership Model. (Source: Education Systems and Design, Inc., Westport, Conn., 1978. Reprinted by permission.)

listen, and try to understand. Out of that concern and understanding the manager may then make suggestions, give feedback, and in one way or another assert his or her position. Thus, the process of caring about others, valuing their resources and information (when one is not denying or denigrating one's own capacity), leads toward interactive behavior where one also gives information and expresses feelings. Finally, many managers are able to integrate Assertive and Responsive behavior—at times emphasizing one or the other—and in the long run develop an interactive, problem-solving leadership style. The range of possibilities in the Assertive and Responsive modes needs to be understood in order for one to maximize leadership effectiveness.

THE ASSERTIVE-RESPONSIVE HIERARCHIES

The general strategies of Assertiveness and Responsiveness can be broken down into components, into tactics and techniques. Each of these sets of behaviors can be arranged in a hierarchy.

The four components of the Assertiveness hierarchy are:

1. Giving information,
2. Expressing a need or want,
3. Persuading or pointing out benefits,
4. Controlling or pointing out negative consequences.

These components are arranged in ascending order. The hierarchy reflects an increasing effort on the part of one individual to have impact on another and to shape the outcomes of a given situation.

Similarly, the Responsiveness hierarchy has four components:

1. Seeking information,
2. Showing understanding,
3. Modifying behavior (your own),
4. Changing behavior (your own).

The hierarchy is arranged in ascending order, reflecting the individual's readiness to respond to or be shaped by the views of others.

Combining Assertiveness and Responsiveness

These Assertive and Responsive approaches can be combined in a variety of ways. First, you can use any of the Assertive modes without including a Responsive component. Conversely, you can use any of the Responsive modes without an assertion. Finally, any of the Assertive comments can be combined with any of the Responsive comments.

Each of these strategies is described more fully below and additional examples are provided to clarify each of the patterns of behavior.

Assertive Behavior You can give information, express wants, persuade, or point out negative consequences in order to produce a result, without denying your own rights and resources or the rights and resources of others. Emphasis, in the Assertive mode, is on your own resources; the goal is to have an impact on surrounding situations or individuals. Assertive behavior does not include a request for information or other overt responsiveness. Here are examples of Assertive behavior:

1. *Giving information:* I haven't received an increase in the last 18 months.
2. *Expressing a need or a want:* I want a raise.
3. *Persuading:* I have been doing a good job and getting good results and I feel by taking on more responsibility I can increase the effectiveness of our organization. I would like to move ahead and have an opportunity to make more money.
4. *Controlling* (points out negative consequences): I have been working hard and I have been getting good results. If I don't move ahead pretty soon, I am going to start looking for another job.

Note again that none of the Assertive statements are putdowns of another person, none are Aggressive even though at some point the individual seems to push pretty hard for what he or she wants. Note, too, that none of the statements includes a Responsive component. There is no request for information, no solicitation, no showing of understanding of the other person's point of view. This does not make the statements bad or wrong. It simply underlines the fact that they are Assertive with no specific Responsive component.

Responsive Behavior A second strategy is one that emphasizes responsiveness and includes no Assertive component. Here is a set of examples of Responsive behavior. Assume for this illustration that a manager and subordinate have been talking over a raise and the manager has pointed out that the subordinate is at the top of the rate range and that an increase will not be granted. The subordinate responds:

1. *Seeks information:* I would like to know more about how you see my performance and what I need to do to obtain an increase.
2. *Shows understanding:* I understand that you feel the rate structure prevents you from granting me an increase.
3. *Modifies behavior* (your own): Based on the fact that I am at the top of the rate range, I understand that it is difficult to obtain an increase, but I do want to know how to get ahead.
4. *Changes behavior* (your own): Well, now that I fully understand the rate structure and how it works, I agree that it is not possible for you to

give me an increase and I will not continue to push for one in my present job category.

Again note that all of these statements are Responsive to the boss without denying the subordinate's rights and resources. In no case does the subordinate put him/herself down. There is also an opportunity with the Responsive mode to move into an Assertive statement. For example, the last statement can be converted into an assertion: "I understand now that I can not get an increase while I am in this rate range so I want to discuss with you how I can move to a higher-rated job." Now the individual has combined responsiveness with assertiveness and that moves us to the third category of behavior.

Assertive–Responsive Behavior

You can combine one or more of the statements in the Assertive and Responsive hierarchies to produce an interactive exchange with another individual. Thus, in a given statement you can assert your own position and also seek out or respond to the position of another. The two hierarchies of statements can be combined in any arrangement in order to produce an interactive, problem-solving response.

Here is a set of examples showing all of the alternatives in a situation in which a manager talks to an employee who has been late rather frequently. The employee has recently been assigned to a new position.

Give information: I noted that you were five minutes late today.

Seek information: What happened to cause you to be late?

Express a want: You were late. I want you to be on time in the future.

Show understanding: I realize that there are problems on your new job that may affect your lateness record. Let's talk over the situation.

Persuade: If you are on time in the future it will increase your chances of getting ahead.

Modify behavior: I have the feeling that your work is not satisfying to you and this may affect your lateness. Perhaps we should spend more time going over your new job.

Control: If you are late again you will be subject to disciplinary action.

Change behavior: I can see that your new job is causing some problems. One possibility is that I could assign you to something else or we could work out a new schedule. Let's talk it over.

Note that with slight modifications any of these statements could stand alone or any Assertive statement could be combined with any Responsive statement. For example:

Give information: "I noted that you were five minutes late today." *Seek information:* "What happened?"

or

Express a want or goal: "You were late. I want you to be on time in the future." *Show understanding:* "I realize that this is a new assignment and it may be causing some problems so let's talk the situation over."

It is important to recognize that as one moves up the Assertive hierarchy, one is not crossing over into Aggressive behavior. Similarly, as one moves up the Responsive hierarchy, one is not being Nonassertive.

Here's an example of a strong assertion by a manager pointing out negative consequences without aggressiveness (no putdown) combined with a highly Responsive statement which does not deny the manager's rights or resources.

Assertive-controlling: "You and I have reviewed your performance frequently and have set some agreed-upon goals. In each case these goals have not been reached. Therefore, you cannot continue in your present assignment and this will mean a reduction in salary."

Responsive-change behavior: "I realize that you were promoted to this job before you had had a chance to get field experience and that may be why you are having trouble. I want to work out a plan with you for your new assignment so you can get the experience you need and get another opportunity to increase your responsibilities and your income."

LEADERSHIP— PROBLEM SOLVING

The foregoing illustrations indicate the range of initiatives and responses that are available to a leader as he or she interacts with others in attempting to achieve results operating within the top half of the Leadership Model. There are many leadership situations in which effectiveness can be equated with the leader's ability to engage people in solving problems and making decisions in which Assertive-Responsive behavior, in combination, is desirable. This does not preclude the need or desirability of utilizing a more controlling and persuasive approach, or a more responsive mode when the situation requires these alternatives. Thus, the effective manager often gives an opinion, expresses goals, and sets objectives. He/she also seeks out opinions and is subject to the influence of others. In some cases the leader may choose to make decisions independently and to push for results. In other instances he/she may choose to rely on the expertise or experience of others. In subsequent chapters some of the advantages and limitations of these various modes will be dealt with in more detail. First, however, the lower half of the circle— Aggressive and Nonassertive behavior—will be explored further.

AGGRESSION AND NON-ASSERTIVENESS

Just as Assertive and Responsive behavior can be broken down into components, shades of difference between the various modes of Aggressive behavior and Nonassertive behavior can be identified. It is important in passing to note that Aggressive and Nonassertive behavior have one thing in common: they are moving away from a two-way flow of information or influence. They are not interactive or problem-solving responses. Thus, they cannot be integrated or combined as was the case with Assertive and Responsive behavior. The specific behaviors associated with each of these strategies or modes of action are described below.

Aggressive Behavior

1. *Patronizing:* When one treats another with condescension one is showing low regard for the other's resources and this is a form of aggressiveness: "You are new on this job and I really don't expect too much of you. Don't worry, you will learn and I will help you when you get in trouble."

   (In contrast, note the more Assertive way of dealing with this same issue: "This is a new job and I am sure there are quite a few things that you will want to look into and learn more about. I will work with you in clarifying areas where further skills or knowledge may be useful to you in order to accomplish the tasks of the job and to achieve your personal goals.")

2. *Shows contempt:* Contempt is a deeper shading of patronization and condescension. It not only shows low regard for the resources of others but tends to be scornful or demeaning. For example, "A woman just doesn't have the temperament to handle an executive job."

3. *Putdowns or attacks:* These patterns are overtly hostile and abrasive. They take one of several forms. When you are being Aggressive, you:

   Ascribe negative motives to others: "You are all out for yourself" or "You don't care—you're impossible."

   Generalize negatively about the other: "You young people are all alike" or "Women don't understand technical problems."

   Become abusive or name-calling: "You are stupid," "Why don't you grow up," "You'll have to learn that I will not put up with immature behavior."

Nonassertive Mode

1. *Accommodation:* When one gives up a piece of what he/she really believes in order to fit in with others, that person has moved into the nonassertive or relinquishing mode. Often, the difference between responsiveness and nonassertiveness is a matter of the underlying feelings and beliefs of the people involved. In general, however, when one quickly takes blame and accompanies it with a tone of self-derision or inappropriate flattery, it becomes clear that accommodation is occurring: "Well, now that I have thought it over I can see that I was pretty stupid to try to get the job done the way I was approaching it. You cer-

tainly have a lot more experience than I and believe me, I am going to be careful and try to do things the way you want them done. I hope you will be patient—I really want to learn.''

2. *Self-pitying:* Often Nonassertive behavior in addition to being self-demeaning is self-pitying and often includes an apology when one is not called for.

   For example, manager to subordinate: "I'm so loaded down I haven't been able to spend much time with you. I haven't had time to breathe in the last couple of weeks. I'm sorry I haven't been able to give you more help but believe me, I need your support. This whole project is getting to be a little too much for me.''

3. *Self-putdowns:* The clearest and most obvious Nonassertive behavior is when one demeans oneself: "I'm not very smart" or "I don't think I can do this without your help," etc. The only difficulty in being clear about this kind of behavior is that at times people are honestly identifying a limitation or lack of knowledge within themselves which can be a straightforward assertion: "I've been working on this project and I realize that my lack of training in mathematics means that I won't be able to solve the problem without some aid from others.''

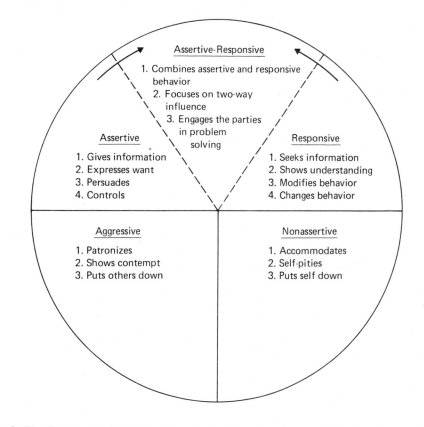

Fig. 2. The Leadership Model. (Source: Educational Systems and Designs, Westport, Conn., 1978. Reprinted by permission.)

It is usually possible to discriminate between Nonassertive self-putdowns and straightforward assertions of one's own limitations or lack of knowledge. Typically, the Nonassertive self-putdown has a self-demeaning, self-pitying quality. It is often volunteered when it is irrelevant and unnecessary and it usually communicates the feeling that the speaker is somehow weak, limited, or incapable of helping him/herself.

These various shades of Aggressive and Nonassertive behavior fill out the basic strategies shown in the Leadership Model (Fig. 2).

SUMMARY An essential step in improving your effectiveness is to be aware of the alternatives that are available as you work with people to achieve results. The Leadership Model is designed to make these alternatives clear and specific. Thus, as you clarify your current mode of behavior and begin examining alternatives you are in a better position to make choices as to how you want to behave. However, in order to act upon your choices—in order to translate your resources into effective and desired action—it is necessary to get in touch with and draw upon capacities that may be dormant or underutilized. Your feelings are critical resources which make it possible for you to pursue your goals. In order to act in new and more effective ways you need to get in touch with and utilize your emotions. The next chapter focuses on the role of feelings in the development of leadership effectiveness.

Getting in Touch with Your Feelings

FEELINGS AS RESOURCES Your feelings energize you. Anger and anxiety mobilize your resources in preparation for action. Creative tensions move you to build and grow. Fear sharpens your awareness of your environment, makes it possible for you to identify dangerous situations and to prepare yourself to deal with them. Affection and concern for others propel you toward affirmative, constructive action in respect to others.

If your goal is to be more Assertive, it is necessary to be in touch with your A feelings; that is, those urges, drives, and emotions that are action-oriented and which push you toward reaching out to the environment, creating new initiatives, standing up for your rights, and defending yourself.

If you wish to be more Responsive, it's important to be in touch with your R feelings: your feelings of compassion and concern, your desire to relate to others, which make it possible for you to tune in to the environment, to listen and to become a part of a family, group, or organization, and to form intimate and caring relationships.

You need to be in touch with, or reach, the full range of your feelings in order to develop the full range of your leadership capacity. All of your feelings are resources—they keep you informed as to what's happening within you, they let you know how the world is affecting you.

Awareness of your R feelings and of the long-term consequences of your own behavior enable you to act on your A drives assertively. Awareness of your A feelings enables you to maintain your identity even as you respond to the needs of others. You will not be Aggressive if you are comfortable with yourself and in touch with the feelings of others. You will not act non-assertively if you value your own resources, if you are self-possessed and feel capable of dealing with those around you.

Going Out of Control Clearly, if any one feeling dominates your total being, becomes the sole or major source of all of your actions, if it gets out of control, it may immobilize you or lead you into ineffective action. For example, fear or anxiety can become so intense that you are unable to act. Anger and rage can cause you to attack others. Your need for affection and for being part of the group can cause you to deny your own self-assertive needs and to compromise your beliefs.

In the final analysis, everyone knows that he or she cannot function without drawing upon the surrounding world and the people in it. Nor can one move forward without drive, energy, and, as needed, self-protective behavior. By being in touch with both your A feelings and resources *and* your R feelings and resources you can develop a balanced, integrated approach to leadership and personal effectiveness.

GETTING IN TOUCH WITH YOUR A RESOURCES

The essential difference between Aggressive and Assertive behavior is that aggression involves putting others down and Assertive behavior does not. Both kinds of behavior stem, in part, from Aggressive feelings. Both modes of action are aimed at influencing the world, shaping events, and defending one's rights and individuality. Both involve acting on drives and feelings which are often seen as destructive. The critical difficulty in being able to act on your A feelings is that there is often confusion as to the true nature of aggression.

Most psychologists agree that Aggressive *feelings and drives* include a wide range of action-oriented emotions: anger; creative energies; the need for power, self-protection, and self-assertion; and the urge to grow and to prevail.[1,2]

What is needed is an awareness of the totality of your A feelings and the capacity to get in touch with and utilize them. There is clearly nothing wrong with having creative drives, a desire to build, to grow, to influence the world around you. However, there is also nothing wrong with being in touch with your need and capacity to overcome obstacles, to break down or destroy inappropriate and outmoded structures or patterns of thought, and to protect your own interests.

Most people have little difficulty in accepting and dealing with their desire to create, build, and grow. Difficulty most often occurs in coping with those Aggressive feelings that mobilize you to defend yourself or that may have a destructive component.

You cannot deny your own Aggressive feelings, including anger and hostility. You can choose to find ways of responding effectively when you are being attacked. Similarly, you can choose to find ways of appropriately managing your own desires to prevail. There are three conditions which must be fulfilled if aggression is to be dealt with effectively. It is necessary to:

1. Acknowledge that aggression exists.

2. Admit to your own feelings of aggression; in other words, own up.

3. Clarify the distinction between feeling Aggressive and behaving aggressively.

Aggression Exists

Not only do people feel Aggressive, they often behave aggressively. People compete with each other. In their desire to get ahead they sometimes step on one another, put each other down. Many institutions and groups are in conflict. They may have significantly differing goals. Union and management organizations often attack each other. Consumer advocates attack corporations and government agencies. Some government agencies attack big business while others are attacking those in the community who attack big business. The point is that aggression is all around us—not simply the engagement of people and groups in trying to solve problems, but real aggression, such as attacks, invective, putdowns, attempts to embarrass or demean other individuals or other institutions. It all seems obvious but strangely a large number of individuals deny the existence of aggression within their own institutions or in their relationships with others. Many deny the fact that they have Aggressive feelings or any need to shape or dominate others. Conversely, there are those who deny that they have been aggressed upon. They claim they are tough and really are unaware of ever being put down.

If one is to deal with aggression effectively, the first and inescapable requirement is simply the admission that aggression is a fact of individual and organizational life. This does not justify Aggressive behavior. It simply means that every human being who is operating in any social context comes in contact with people who feel and act aggressively. The feeling may be very personal: "I'd like to get even with my boss for the way in which he has treated me." Or it may be very general: "We in the union know that management is against us and we have to do everything we can to keep on top and to demonstrate to our members that management is deceitful and dishonest."

In any case, these feelings may be converted into action. Two organization members competing for the same job may go so far as to lie regarding each other's performance or to take manipulative or covert steps to make the other look bad. There is certainly ample evidence in our political campaigns and in international affairs that at all levels of our society, people are willing to lie, cheat, manipulate, and figuratively and literally kill others in order to sustain or improve their own positions. And so most of the people around us at one time or another, and in varying degrees, feel Aggressive and *may* act on that feeling.

Admitting that aggression is present and that there are people out there who have Aggressive feelings toward us may be disquieting. It is even more difficult to take in the idea that people we like, people who are close to us, people who clearly have a concern for us, are also capable of aggression toward us. There are times when wives, husbands, and children have Aggressive feelings toward each other and have a desire to act upon them. Parents at times do try to embarrass, put down, or in some way demean their own children. Conversely, children often have subtle ways of making parents look bad or feel badly about their own behavior. Similarly, subordinates have ways of "getting" their bosses, and the boss may find it necessary at times to act upon some of his own desires to look better than the subordinate or to attack some aspect of the subordinate's performance or behavior. It is important to own up to the fact that your friends, your boss, your subordinates at times feel Aggressive toward you and at times may act on those Aggressive feelings. Only then can you deal with their feelings effectively.

You, Too, Feel Aggression

There is a second requirement for dealing with aggression. Not only must one admit that it exists in the surrounding world, not only must one face the fact that friends, associates, bosses, and subordinates may have Aggressive feelings toward those with whom they work, but also one must admit that he or she has Aggressive feelings toward others. There is research and psychological proof on this issue but the fact is more easily proven by simply referring to one's own past experience. A husband or wife who has not had the desire to put down, embarrass, or verbally (sometimes physically) attack his or her spouse is indeed rare. And there are few subordinates who, at one time or another, have not felt Aggressive toward a boss. And certainly everyone has experienced Aggressive feelings when being cut off in traffic or pushed aside while waiting in line. And at a given moment, even though no action may be taken, the desire to attack is often strong: "At this moment I want to demean, diminish, or wipe out that other person." There are some fairly typical defenses that organization members use to deny some of these feelings and it's important to check these out as one explores his or her own capacity to admit to and deal with aggression. Here are two examples.

1. Feelings are unimportant.

   Many managers take the stance that the important thing is getting the job done, and being concerned about how other people feel or being sensitive to attacks upon yourself are simply distractions from the job. The fact is that people do have feelings, they do get impatient, angry, upset, and sensitive. This is simply an undeniable fact of the human situation. To act as though all that mattered was the "bottom line" ignores the fact that the bottom line is achieved by people who are committed, concerned, interested, stimulated, challenged, and involved. When people are involved, when people are intensely working toward achievement, the psychological reality is that interruptions, distractions, criticisms often create an immediate feeling of anger and aggression. To be shocked or unprepared for the Aggressive feelings of others is naive. To be unprepared to defend yourself against aggression is to devalue your own worth and your personal rights and integrity.

2. Aggressive feelings are not normal.

   Unfortunately, throughout your life you have been told to deny your Aggressive feelings. The underlying assumption is that anger, Aggressive feelings and hostile feelings are bad. In fact, they are not bad—they are human feelings. They are deeply connected to humankind's past, woven into both your psychological and physical being. Fear, anger, and aggression are not isolated psychological developments. There is a basic and essential mind-body connection. When you face a real or imagined threat, adrenalin pumps into the system. The human organism becomes more ready for fight or flight. In effect, nature provides human beings with complex mechanisms for defending themselves. These mechanisms may trigger attacks or they may trigger withdrawal or flight. Simply stated, then, if you are attacked or if you are striving toward a goal, it is human, normal, natural, and physically and psychologically appropriate for you to mobilize your resources to defend yourself or to move forward. Accompanying that mobilization of resources are Aggressive feelings. To deny those feelings is to deny one's own humanness.

Feeling and Doing   Thus, aggression exists within everyone. We feel it. The fact is that being able to feel is a prerequisite to being able to act. Denial or distortion of the feeling leads toward a distorted act. Recognizing the feeling and being able to channel it appropriately is the key to effectiveness as a human being and as a leader.

When Jimmy Carter was campaigning for the presidency, he took part in an interview in which he discussed his beliefs and contrasted them with his feelings. He pointed out that he always tried to behave righteously but that he had feelings that were not in line with his values. In the process of discussing this dilemma, he shocked millions of Americans when he admitted to lust in his heart. His point, and the key insight that is essential to becoming more effective as a leader, is the recognition that being aware of the feeling does not mean that one will act on the feeling. Being in touch with your feelings makes it possible for you to utilize them constructively. In fact, it is because of your feelings, your anger, your intensity about a given issue or situation that you are able to mobilize and channel your own resources so as to act effectively. And the hard, psychological fact is that when you deny your Aggressive feelings, very often the resultant behavior is more damaging than if the feeling had been admitted. When you deny your desire to win or to get ahead, you cut off some of your own energy. When you refuse to feel your aggression or to find an outlet for it, feelings build up and may become explosive. Bach and Goldberg clarify and dramatize the dangers of withheld agression by pointing out that it is socially and physically hazardous:

Indeed, it is the aggressive-phobic society demanding the suppression of negative feelings that is most vulnerable to the bizarre outbursts of violence that have become a part of our culture. . . . Society will be far less vulnerable when it has recognized and acepted the normal, natural build-up and need for constructive release of anger and hostility in all people.[3]

However, being in touch with your Aggressive feelings does not mean that you can simply let go with explosive anger, destructive rage, or immobilizing anxiety. A feelings must be acknowledged and integrated with other feelings —concern for others, enlightened self-interest, fear of the consequences of uncontrolled hostility. This integration and awareness result in appropriate controls rather than overcontrol (denial of or inability to act on your feelings) or undercontrol (self-indulgent and ineffective outbursts of anger or rage).

The idea that the feelings and drives associated with aggression can be either overcontrolled or undercontrolled, and that in either case negative consequences may occur, has been studied in group situations, dealing with persons who have serious difficulties in coping with their own angry feelings. One clinician points out:

They (overcontrolled individuals) have been taught not to express anger, and keep their anger to themselves until it reaches volcanic proportions at which point they might "blow," possibly engaging in violent behavior. Others may show a pattern of undercontrol *wherein only minimal instigation to anger results in instant aggression.*[4]

Owning Up In any case, the first step in acting assertively and in appropriately controlling and channeling your Aggressive energies is to recognize your true feelings. As a quick check on your A feelings, consider these statements. Try saying each of them several times aloud; connect with your A drives.

I like "doing"—I want to create, to initiate action.

I want to get ahead.

I like to win.

When people put me down, I feel angry.

I am a unique individual.

I can make things happen.

I want to be heard, to have impact on the world around me.

I have the right to pursue my goals and interests.

I have resources that other people need and value.

It is natural and appropriate to want to prevail, to be unique, to defend yourself. It is also natural to want to have impact, to create, to be heard. At times you have to defend yourself against the overprotection or stifling concern of parents or helpful bosses. Sometimes you have to take a stand against the Aggressive behavior of colleagues, competitiors, or those in higher authority. In order to act effectively, you must acknowledge and utilize all of your resources—your creative and your destructive feelings belong to you. Owning up to these feelings does not mean you have to express them. The goal is to channel your Aggressive drives and feelings—both your creative and destructive urges—in ways that are effective and consistent with your own goals and values. In part this can be done by finding ways to act on your feelings and beliefs assertively. The second requirement for effectively channeling your energies constructively lies in your ability to tune into the environment, the people around you.

DRAWING UPON YOUR RESPONSIVE FEELINGS

There has been confusion about aggression because of difficulty in accepting the idea that it includes *both* creative and destructive drives and that in the final analysis, Aggressive feelings do not have to lead to Aggressive acts. Similarly, there is confusion about the caring, Responsive components of your feelings and behavior.

At The Beginning, Responsiveness

When we think of our heritage, of our ancestors, we think of people who were Aggressive. Primitive people are usually portrayed as fighters—killing animals, combating the elements, carving, chopping, building, and shaping. A closer look at our evolution reveals that early humans spent most of their time trying to flow with the environment, to be responsive. In *The Ascent of Man*,[5] Jacob Bronowski points out that the earliest primitive people had no tools or implements; they built nothing. They found ways of fitting into the world around them, of using the natural resources of the environment without modifying or shaping them in any way. In fact, Bronowski points out that the major turning point in evolution was when people began to use their hands to shape things, when they began to cut into their environment and have an impact on the world around them. So at the beginning the key to survival was the ability to use and respond to the environment, to react and flow with the powerful forces over which primitive people had no control. It was later that people began to assert themselves, to establish themselves as more than simply a cog in the wheel of nature.

It is also clear in the evolution of families and groups that those who survive are those who develop some capacity to care for each other. Early in the evolutionary process the young who were not cared for by their parents did not survive. The noncaring parents did not procreate. Our primal ancestors learned to form groups, to warn each other of danger, and later to cooperate in the development of agriculture and in increasingly complex, collaborative ventures. And so the desire and capacity to fit in with the world, to be a part of a larger group, to care for and cooperate with others are at least as deeply rooted as are instincts to fight, to remain independent, and to compete with others.

The Nature of Responsiveness

The roots of our Responsive feelings are complex. On the one hand, our personal and collective histories have taught us that in some areas and in some situations we must cooperate in order to survive. If someone is warning us of danger or providing us with information we need, it's clear that the capacity to listen and to understand may be critical to our own survival. We know, too, that if someone wants to join with us to improve our capacities to grow, to succeed, or to defend ourselves, then it is also desirable and useful to be open, Responsive, and available for that type of cooperative endeavor. The ability to hear other people's ideas, to accept warnings from others, and to be able to cooperate in useful joint ventures is not simply a function of caring but, rather, a function of one's own enlightened self-interest.

There is also, however, a dimension of ourselves that is rooted in a caring concern for others, not motivated by simple self-interest. Clearly, parents make personal sacrifices for their children, and friends have at times given their lives for each other. Starving people do at times share their bread. And so, deep within us, out of our primitive past, out of our experience as children and parents, out of our experience as members of families, tribes, and organizations, we do have a capacity to care, to be supportive. Love, compassion, and affection are as genuine and deeply rooted as acquisitiveness, self-interest, and competitiveness.

There is a third dimension to our responsive nature. Often we behave responsively out of our sense of inadequacy and fear. We need to be liked or loved. Just as we have a need to be supportive, to be cooperative, to be concerned with those around us, so we have a need to get support, affection, and cooperation from others.

Feeling Is Not Doing   You can feel affection, concern, and empathy for others without acting in ways that are self-destructive or organizationally ineffective. You can recognize and feel your strong desire to be liked by others but that does not mean that you will compromise your principles, demean yourself, or violate sound policy in order to win the desired affection. Being aware of what you feel makes it possible for you to make a conscious and appropriate choice of behavior. It is when you act on your own need to be liked without recognizing your true feelings that you get in trouble.

For example, consider the son who strives to be a doctor to fill his father's expectations and then realizes that medicine is not really meaningful to him; or the manager who is tough with people, cuts them off, behaves as a hatchet man, not because this is the way in which he wants to behave but because this is a way in which he thinks he will win the respect or acceptance of his boss. Often the difficult ingredient in these situations is not that the individual is aware of his need for affection or respect from others but rather that he is unaware of it. He proceeds in ways which are unfulfilling, self-defeating, or even illegal or unethical without knowing that he is behaving this way because of his need for support, affection, or respect. The way in which one can get caught in self-deluding behavior is well described in John Dean's book *Blind Ambition*. Dean admits that late in the game he recognized that much of what he was doing was for approbation, for respect from others. He sums up his own plight when he says: "Slowly, steadily, I would climb toward the moral abyss of the President's inner circle until I finally fell into it, thinking I had made it to the top just as I began to realize I had actually touched bottom."[6] If he had been in touch with the fact that a great deal of his behavior was both self-deluding and self-demeaning, then he might have been in a better position to make more appropriate choices.

We know that we are strongly influenced by our desire to please the boss, to be liked by important people, or to satisfy the expectations of parents or others in authority. If you can be clear about these feelings, they can then be understood, channeled, and controlled. The danger is not in psychological truth. The danger is in psychological lies. The statements which follow are expressions of urges and drives that contribute to Responsive behavior. Read them aloud several times; connect with your R feelings.

> I want to be liked; it is important for me to be seen as a decent, reasonable individual.
>
> I care about people.
>
> I do not want to see others hurt or destroyed.
>
> I want to be involved with other individuals and groups.
>
> I want to be in tune with others, feel some commonality and universality with the people around me.
>
> I want to understand and relate to others.
>
> I need affection and support from others.
>
> Other people have resources that I need and value.

Once again, it may be true that you or others you know do not act on these feelings and, in fact, may rarely experience them. But there is an abundance of historical, social, and psychological evidence (and for most of us, a great deal of personal experience) which indicates that these feelings are present, that they are natural. It is unnatural for you to be isolated, invulnerable, out of touch with the individuals and groups around you. Your needs for affiliation and affection can be ignored, or they can become all-encompassing and destroy your individuality and integrity. More appropriately, however, they can be utilized and built upon to form relationships and to survive and grow in an interdependent world.

Thus, your R feelings and needs can produce Responsive behavior that is useful and interactive and that moves you toward solving problems and maintaining your own strength and self-esteem. Or these same needs and drives can push you in the direction of denying your own beliefs and going along with others, or becoming Nonassertive, thus avoiding any genuine risk or involvement.

Nonassertive behavior is often confused with Responsive behavior. Managers often justify soft, relinquishing behavior by describing it as caring or Responsive. Many subordinates permit themselves to be put down or exploited by their boss on the basis that they want to be *nice*. The fact is that Nonassertive behavior, by definition, is not motivated by a desire to cooperate; it is not a function of genuine caring. Nonassertive behavior is defensive; it denies one's own knowledge, one's own needs and drives. Nonassertive behavior is often an indication that the individual is not involved with or is afraid of his or her own A feelings.

Responsive behavior occurs when one is sufficiently in touch with one's own A resources and capacity to defend oneself to feel safe in admitting a need for the support and affection of others and the need to draw on the resources of others in order to solve problems and get things done.

STAYING IN TOUCH   The emphasis in the chapters that follow will be on *action*. However, periodically it's useful to review the basic feelings that energize that action. Therefore, as you explore specific techniques and procedures for increasing your Assertive and Responsive behavior—if that is the choice you have made —you will be provided periodically with opportunities to check out your feelings and the degree to which you can move into action with conviction and power.

NOTES

1. For example, Bach and Goldberg define aggression as including ". . . anger, resentment, and rage; self-assertion; open, leveling confrontations; the active reaching out to situations and people. . ." See George R. Bach and Herb Goldberg, *Creative Aggression: A Guide to Assertive Living*, New York: Avon, 1974, p. 83.

2. Latner points out that Aggressive behavior includes creative activity as well as hostile or destructive activity. He says, "In the process of living, we must create and destroy. These processes are aggressive ones." Joel Latner, *The Gestalt Therapy Book*, New York: Bantam Books, 1973, p. 36.

3. George R. Bach and Herb Goldberg, *Creative Aggression: A Guide to Assertive Living*, New York: Avon, 1974.

4. Robert E. Alberti, *Assertiveness*, San Luis Obispo, Calif.: Impact, 1977, p. 87.

5. Jacob Bronowski, *The Ascent of Man*, Boston/Toronto: Little, Brown, 1973.

6. John Dean, *Blind Ambition*, New York: Simon & Schuster, 1976, p. 31.

6

Becoming More Assertive

FROM FEELING TO DOING

Your need and desire to act, to create, to survive, and to defend yourself are the energizing resources that can move you from where you are to where you want to be. However, those feelings must be channeled into action that is effective and fulfilling. Musicians learn scales, golfers find ways of improving their swing, and engineers and scientists learn theorems, the scientific method, and the how-to's of their field. Guidelines, prescriptions, formulations, routines, drills, and systems are necessary ingredients in the learning process. If they reduce creativity and spontaneity they are ineffective. If these procedures move you toward fuller utilization of your unique resources and toward development of your capacities, they become facilitating mechanisms for getting where you want to be. They can't take the place of your own energy, drive, and commitment. They can, however, help you translate your feelings and drives into effective action.

The guidelines that follow provide how-to's and procedures for practicing assertive skills.

GUIDELINES FOR ASSERTIVENESS

Here are six basic suggestions that can lead you toward a more Assertive leadership style.

1. Identify and use the full range of Assertive techniques (that is, use the assertiveness hierarchy).
2. Be expressive; let other people know how you feel and where you stand.
3. Maintain a goal-oriented approach.
4. Be clear.
5. Avoid putdowns.
6. Integrate the content of what you do with how you do it (integrate substance and style).

Each of these components of Assertive behavior will be reviewed briefly.

Using the Full Range of Assertive Techniques

The assertiveness hierarchy (presented earlier) spells out the specific content of Assertive statements.

Assertive statements:

Give information.

Express wants or goals.

Point out benefits (persuade).

Point out negative consequences (control).

Each of these guidelines at every level of the hierarchy can be executed most effectively when a basic set of Assertive skills is applied.

Assertive skills

Input, not pressure. The most basic skill for assertiveness involves using only the amount of information or influence—including facts, feelings, and opinions—that is needed to achieve your goal. In general, when you introduce unneeded pressure into your attempts to influence others you reduce your effectiveness. The two critical ground rules for avoiding inappropriate or premature pressure, which, in turn, produces resistance, are:

1. Stay at the lower levels of the hierarchy at the start of an interaction.
2. Avoid value judgments until basic information is on the table.

Here are examples of what to avoid and how to improve the flow of communication *early* in a discussion.

Use of pressure—not O.K.	*Make inputs—O.K.*
You haven't done a very good job on costs and if you don't improve I'll have to hold up your increase. (A value judgment of "good" and a negative sanction. The other person may well become defensive, probably not in a good frame of mind to solve problems.)	Costs are up in your operation. I want to work out a plan with you to deal with the cost situation. (Gives information, no value judgment, stays low level, and expresses want.)
If you reduce costs you will be more apt to get an increase. (This is a persuasive statement; it begins to sell before the problem has been aired. This may cause the other to give in rather than express real problems or to fight against the pressure.)	Let's review cost performance and determine if any action needs to be taken. (A two-way process is proposed without pressure or sanctions. Problem solving is encouraged, without creating defensiveness.)
I am disgusted with your performance; if you can't solve the problem we will get someone who can. (A significant escalation, up the hierarchy into aggression, negative sanctions, and negative emotional value statements: disgusted, can't solve it.)	I am very concerned about costs. I want to understand what has been happening and reduce costs. (This is still at the lower levels of the hierarchy, no sanctions. It is a relatively strong statement including a felt expression of concern. It may produce some pressure; however, it is basically still an invitation to problem-solve.)

In review: All of the responses above demonstrate how to make inputs and avoid pressure in early stages of an interaction. As the interaction continues, or if results don't improve, you may need to escalate—point out benefits or negative sanctions and make value judgments.

From the general to the specific. The second set of assertiveness skills requires the capacity to maintain a balance between being suitably flexible and being either equivocal on the one hand or rigid on the other. The most typical manifestation of rigidity is becoming too specific too soon, thus closing off discussion and open, two-way interaction. Typically, rigidity is caused by a desire to control the environment. The usual cause of equivocation is an inappropriate concern with being a nice person, often coupled with an unwillingness to be open or straight concerning how you really feel. The goal—early in the interaction—is to be firm *and* to keep options open. Here are examples:

Situation: You have decided to ask for a raise.

Rigid—not O.K.	*Equivocal—not O.K.*	*Straight—O.K.*
I have been getting good results. I deserve a raise and I want an increase by the first of the year. (Too specific, too soon.)	I think I have been doing a good job. I have certainly been trying. I'd appreciate it if you'd consider an increase for me. (Wishy-washy.)	I want to discuss an increase in salary. (Clear expression of purpose; open up two-way flow.)

At later stages of an interaction or relationship the manager may appropriately become more specific.

Situation: You have to deny a salary increase to a subordinate who hasn't met agreed-upon standards and goals. The subordinate feels he/she deserves an increase. Assume you've had previous goal-setting and performance discussions.

Rigid—not O.K.	*Equivocal—not O.K.*	*Straight—O.K.*
I have analyzed your performance. You are not up to standard. There will be no increases. ("I" centered, no room for dialogue.)	Each of us has to use his or her own judgment in assessing performance. Much as we try to be objective, there are often differing viewpoints. I can't, in good conscience, justify an increase—maybe I am misjudging the situation but I have used the facts—and as I see it, you do not meet standards. (Long-winded, defensive.)	You won't be getting an increase this quarter. Specific goals and standards have not been met. We should begin now to plan for the future. (Clear, leaves room to discuss future.)

In review: Managers must make judgments. They may give information, show concern for others, and remain open during early stages of an interaction. However, once a judgment is made or a feeling is expressed, it should be straightforward—neither rigid nor equivocal.

Assertive Skills— Practice

In the following problem situations you are asked to design Assertive statements to deal with each of the issues. Comparative analysis and statements are provided.

Situation 1: A subordinate comes to you with an unexpected request: he/she wants to schedule overtime. You're concerned because overtime costs have been rising over budget. Design an Assertive statement to indicate how you would behave in dealing with the subordinate. (Note: Your first inclination may be to ask a question and that is appropriate. However, for practice you're asked to be Assertive.)

Your statement: _____

_____

_____

_____

_____

Comparative Analysis: This is a new situation. You don't have all the facts. It's best to keep the situation open, to stay general and also to be straightforward regarding your feelings; something like: "We are over budget on overtime. I want to avoid this if we can." Undesirable assertion: "You will have to have a good justification" (creates defensiveness, too specific too soon). "I am sure you can find a way to avoid overtime" (you don't have the facts, you're closing off exchange on a new problem).

Situation 2: You are angry at an associate who criticized your department in the presence of your boss. You feel the criticism was uncalled for and, in any case, should have been dealt with privately. Design an Assertive statement:

_____

_____

_____

_____

_____

Comparative analysis: There is a real temptation to blow off, make threats, or put down the other. It is more useful to be straight about your feeling and to stay at a lower level of the hierarchy; that is, don't make value judgments, don't employ sanctions but give inputs, suggest courses of action. For example: "I was angry when you criticized my group at the staff meeting. I feel strongly that if you have problems with us you should bring them to me privately.'' Undesirable assertion: "If you pull that again I'll start playing the same game,'' (threat) or, "That was a dirty trick" (value judgment).

Situation 3: You want your subordinate to spend more time on supervising and less time doing the work himself/herself. You want him/her to delegate. Assume *you've been talking to him/her for some time* and the subordinate has agreed to let go of some critical tasks. Design an Assertive statement:

_____

_____

_____

_____

_____

Comparative analysis: You have already exchanged information. You can now summarize and be specific (set review dates, times, etc.), and you may choose to close on benefits. For example: "We have agreed you are going to delegate several important tasks to your subordinates. Let's meet in two weeks to see how it has gone. I want to emphasize that the more you apply your managerial capacities, the more ready you are to take one more responsibility some time in the future." Note that it is often appropriate to express how you feel as part of an Assertive statement. Even if your feeling is negative you have a right to express it—it will increase the effectiveness of your communication so long as you don't put yourself or others down. Examples:

Not O.K.	*O.K.*
I was angry. You don't care how much you inconvenience others.	I was angry when you were late for our appointment. I want you to be on time.
I'm scared of appearing before a large audience. I guess I'm just not self-confident enough to handle this.	The idea of appearing before a large audience scares me. I want to practice my speech and get feedback so that I'll be effective.

These brief examples of the assertiveness hierarchy demonstrate that you have choices to make in the manner and sequence in which you present information and move toward increasing your influence in dealing with others. The remaining assertiveness guidelines demonstrate ways in which you can use the hierarchy to advantage.

Be Expressive It is important in building an Assertive mode of behavior to recognize that an expression of feelings is often an important ingredient in impacting upon others. Being expressive means that your communications make contact. This is most apt to occur when you permit your feelings to energize and personalize your message. So showing an excitement and concern and taking personal responsibility for what you're saying enhances your expressiveness and your impact. Some of the obstacles that can stand in the way of expressiveness include: depersonalizing what you have to say, invoking higher authority or third parties, trying to make everything rational and factual, ignoring or dismissing your personal concerns and feelings, using language and expressions that are flat and unemotional. Here are two contrasting examples:

First, an *unexpressive statement:* "As you may know, the home office is interested in achieving better results. It wants people in your position to spend more time on planning and pursuing organizational goals and purposes more systematically. It would be well for you to attend to this matter and to develop a sound plan which will be acceptable to management." (Note the manager never says "I"—he/she does not personalize management nor take responsibility for, nor express his/her feelings.)

Next, an *expressive communication:* "I want to review some of your goals and work with you to clarify departmental plans. We have an opportunity this quarter to do some new and interesting things and to develop programs that will make an impact on the total system." (In this instance the manager takes responsibility him/herself for opening up the topic. The manager indicates an affirmative, positive concern.)

Maintain a Goal-Oriented Approach

As you give information, express wants, persuade, or point out negative consequences for others, it is useful and impactful to use these patterns of the hierarchy as a way of clarifying and moving toward goals. It is also appropriate to express your own needs, wants, and feelings. Even a highly charged, emotional, and somewhat negative situation can be dealt with in a goal-oriented fashion. For example:

"I was very upset at the meeting yesterday when you said some derogatory things about one of your associates who was not present. If you disagree with a specific plan of action, you certainly have every right to express it and I want to hear about it. When an individual is criticized without an opportunity to defend him/herself, others in the group become embarrassed and it detracts from mutual trust. Certainly there are times when each of us gets angry or upset with someone or disagrees with someone. I urge that when that happens, you deal with the person directly and individually and pursue the issue so as to solve the problem." (And so feelings are expressed, negative consequences are discussed, and in some ways the subordinate is being criticized but is not being put down or demeaned. The conversation is moved back toward the question of results.)

Be Clear   In order to be impactful and effective, and in order to be affirmative, Assertive, and straightforward, it is necessary to be clear. The major obstacle to clarity is an unwillingness to acknowledge and act on what you feel. It is often better to get your feelings out on the table, in a nonpunitive way, than to try to make things easy and comfortable for yourself or the other person. And so in order to be clear, to be concise, to be straightforward, the two most important questions are: How do I really feel about this situation? And, How can I express what I feel in a constructive fashion? Here again are a few examples to illustrate the point.

Assume that someone in your group has been late quite often and you're upset by the lateness and somewhat angry about it. If you don't accept this feeling and respond to it, the chances are you will be obscure, formal, or inappropriately harsh in dealing with the problem. And so you might say something like this: "As you know, the policy of our organization dictates that everyone not only is responsible for his or her own job but also has a role to play in the larger organization, and when one individual is not available or is tardy, it disrupts others. The rules must be followed." The fact is that what you really want to say is "I'm upset about your lateness. I want it to stop." You might then add: "Let's discuss what has been happening."

Another more positive example: You are pleased with a subordinate's performance but you don't want to sound saccharine so you mask your warm feeling by saying, "The home office is gratified by the way in which you have been organizing your work. We know that there is still a lot to be done but you are certainly striving for results," etc. What you really mean is, "I'm delighted with the results you've been getting. Everyone up the line is pleased."

Avoid Putdowns   Very often putdowns are utilized when an individual is a little unsure of him/ herself or wants to stay one-up and is afraid that if he/she shows any doubt or anything less than complete assurance, he/she will lose. For example, very often young people who get good grades are criticized, putdown, and embarrassed by their peers. The fact is, their peers are envious, doubtful of their own capacity, uncomfortable or guilty with their own performance, and therefore attack the person who has done well. Similarly, when as a child you were unsure of yourself in a social or classroom situation, you will probably recall a tendency to mock the teacher and attack those who were part of the threatening situation. So when little boys say girls are dumb they say it because they don't have the assurance, the experience, the knowledge, and the esteem to deal with their own feelings about girls.

In analyzing your own communications and attempting to improve them, if you find yourself using putdowns, ask the question, "Is my need to put people down a function of my confidence, self-esteem, and assurance, or is it a sign of self-doubt and lack of assurance?" If the latter is true, awareness of this feeling can then lead you toward a more assertive, nonpunitive mode of behavior.

Integrate Content and Style

If you are truly self-assured, in touch with your own feelings, willing to take responsibility for your own behavior, the chances are good that *what* you say will be consistent with *how* you say it.

Body language, nonverbal content, tone of voice, and the use of positive and affirmative words are all part of your message. They occur as positive components of your message when you are in touch with your feelings and when you channel those feelings assertively. And so your style of delivery is in part a function of what you feel. Although it may at first appear paradoxical, your style of delivery also has an effect upon your feelings. By acting affirmatively, you begin to feel affirmative. Simply by changing your overt behavior, by being more expressive and demonstrative, you build more confidence and feel better about what you're doing. And so body language and other aspects of your style of delivery are not only expressions of what you feel; they also often contribute to a more Assertive, positive, self-confident feeling. Here are some of the steps you can take to integrate an Assertive delivery with an Assertive message, to support and reinforce your own self-confidence and positive impact.

1. *Eye contact:* Make eye contact. Look at people you're talking to. Don't look down. Don't stare or glare.

2. *Body stance:* Stand or sit up firmly rather than in a slouched or withdrawn fashion. Your body and your feelings reinforce each other and in turn support your message.

3. *Gestures:* Use gestures which are natural, comfortable, and compatible with your message. Punching people with your finger or pointing at them or "putting your nose in their face" all have an Aggressive impact. Similarly, shrugging your shoulders, pulling away, averting your eyes are Nonassertive messages.

4. *Tone of voice:* Aggressive behavior is often expressed in loud, harsh, grating tones; Nonassertive behavior often has a whining, apologetic, tentative quality. Straightforward Assertive behavior is firm, the tone of voice is connected with the content and feeling of what's being said.

5. *Tempo of delivery:* It is not unusual for Aggressive expressions to be stated quickly, explosively, phrases often running together. When one is being Nonassertive there are long, inappropriate pauses, redundancies, and a slow tempo of delivery. Assertive behavior tends to be expressed at a fairly rapid tempo but one that is natural and consistent with the individual's behavior in situations in which he or she is comfortable and assured.

6. *Choice of words:* Words and expressions used in Assertive statements are usually positive and active. Saying "I will try to do it," or, "I think

it can be done," are often expressions of an unsure feeling. It is often more appropriate and assertive to say, "I will do it." Perjorative words like stupid, lazy, careless, irresponsible are rarely used in Assertive dialogue.

Excessive apologies and thank-yous are inappropriate, as are words that have a self-demeaning quality. Words like success, achievement, goal, enthusiasm, excitement, and words which connote the same or similar meanings, are most often associated with Assertive behavior. Clearly, one can become pre-occupied with semantics which in some cases may be a trivial issue. On the other hand, if your general feeling tone and choice of expressions is hostile or self-demeaning, this can connote a feeling of aggression or lack of confidence that is neither needed nor intended.

Practice Awareness of the assertiveness hierarchy and some of the methods of delivery and behaviors that can enhance Assertive behavior can aid you in developing a more Assertive style. However, practice is an essential ingredient in the development of Assertive capacity. In Chapter 8 a series of practice situations are provided, but first, in the next chapter, responsive techniques will be outlined.

7

Becoming More Responsive

FROM FEELING TO DOING

Over the last several years a great deal of attention has been paid to taking care of oneself. Self-actualization and feeling good about yourself have become preoccupying concerns at every level of our society. In the rush for self-fulfillment and in the pursuit of individual rights there has been a tendency to lose touch with the fact that achievement and fulfillment must also involve others. In order to feel right about yourself, you often need the understanding, support, and affection of others. In order to get things done, you need to tap the resources of others, to tune into the energy which exists around you. Guidelines, procedures, and techniques for building your Responsive skills are essential to the development of a balanced, effective leadership style.

GUIDELINES FOR RESPONSIVENESS

Guidelines for developing a more Responsive leadership style are outlined below:

1. Identify and utilize the full range of Responsive techniques; that is, use the assertiveness hierarchy.
   a) Seek information.
   b) Show understanding.
   c) Modify behavior.
   d) Change behavior.
2. Tune into the feelings of others.
3. Use goal-oriented responses.
4. Clarify and summarize the feelings and opinions of others.
5. Avoid self-putdowns.
6. Integrate the content of what you do with how you do it (integrate Responsive substance with Responsive style).

Responsive Techniques

Many of the techniques associated with responsiveness require the use of a variety of questioning and listening techniques. Many of these methods are drawn from psychological theories developed by Carl Rogers.[1] Rogers was the first psychologist to identify and dramatize the power of *listening* for solving psychological problems and for providing guidance and counseling. Many of Rogers' methods were combined with other interviewing skills and were gradually moved out of the therapeutic setting into the public and private sectors. Therefore, many of the methods that follow have been available to managers for many years, but it is only in the last ten years or so that they have begun to be applied in day-to-day management and leadership situations.[2]

There are six basic methods that can be utilized to implement the responsiveness guidelines:

1. Direct questions.
2. Overhead or discussion questions.

3. Reflective responses.
4. Interpretive responses.
5. Supportive responses.
6. "Listening" statements.

Direct questions

If you want to find out where someone stands, the simplest and most direct approach is to ask the individual a question. Direct questions are characterized by the fact that they solicit specific information and leave little room for elaboration. Questions such as, "What time did you get in this morning?" "When can I expect that report?" "Are we over budget this month?" "Do you agree?" are typical of direct questions.

Overhead or discussion questions

Overhead or discussion questions provide more opportunity for elaboration and are more apt to produce a two-way flow of information. Such questions as, "Tell me how things have been going?" "What kinds of problems do you foresee in meeting the budget?" "I've noticed you've been late a few times lately. Tell me, what's been happening?" are considered overhead.

Reflective responses

Reflective responses mirror what the other person is saying or feeling. They are most useful in reacting to someone else's comment. Reflective responses take two basic forms:

1. They may simply be a mirror or reflection of the other person's feeling or comment.
2. They may be nonverbal responses indicating your hope that the other person will keep talking and that you are aware and available. Such things as nodding your head, or saying "uh huh," or simply remaining silent may indicate concern without judging the interviewee's response.

Many managers, upon first hearing about reflective or nondirective techniques, can't believe that these techniques are practical. However, thousands of interviewers use the reflective and nondirective methods in order to encourage a flow of communication. Many managers have learned to apply these techniques in connection with performance review or in handling complaints or interpersonal conflicts. The essence of the approach is not that the interviewer restates what another has said but rather that he/she is demonstrating by his/her behavior that he/she is interested in and seeking out the opinions of the other person. Here is a very brief exchange to show how the reflective response works.

Interviewee: Things haven't been going too well lately. I really don't know what's wrong with my department.

Interviewer: I see. You are not too satisfied with things. . . . (Reflective, implying, "tell me more.")

Interviewee: Yes. Our costs are up and the biggest problem seems to be in indirect labor.

Interviewer: Your increased costs are coming primarily from indirect labor. (Reflective)

Interviewee: Yes, but I don't really think that is the basic problem. Somehow the real problem is the attitude some of my people have toward controlling costs.

Interviewer: It looks like an attitude problem then, ... (Reflective, implying "I understand, tell me more.")

Interviewee: Yes, well, my people think the new standard cost system is unworkable. Frankly, I rather agree with them.

This interview is hypothetical but demonstrates common problems in face-to-face communications. Many people hesitate to confront a problem area, particularly if they see the other person (especially the boss) as having a vested interest or a resistance to their own point of view. In this case, apparently the interviewee did not want to come out and say that he/she didn't like the cost system, and the interviewer (boss) was willing to take time to show interest and concern with the interviewee's feelings. Gradually the problem began to be more clear.

Managers do not always have the time or the inclination to use reflective responses. Nevertheless, the reflective response is a tool which need not be the main item in one's set of skills but is an auxiliary method that often opens up discussion when other methods fail.

Interpretive responses   The interpretive response is similar to the reflective response except that the interviewer or manager indicates his/her own analysis of judgment; in effect, the interviewer gives some feedback to the other person. Note that in the reflective response the interviewer adds nothing to what the interviewee has said, whereas the interpretive reaction is one which includes a judgment about what has been going on. For example, the same interview situation used illustratively for demonstrating reflective responses is repeated below, using the interpretive response.

Interviewee: I'm not happy with the way things are going in my department.

Interviewer: Well, yes, I noticed that costs were up and I expect that is one of the things that is bothering you. (Interpretive)

Interviewee: You're right, and indirect labor is getting out of hand.

Interviewer: Well, I can understand that but it seems to me that you are quite upset about this problem, more upset than you normally are when it's simply a matter of controlling or reducing costs. (Interpretive)

Interviewee: Well, I guess what bothers me is that my people don't have much confidence in the new system and it makes me a little uncomfortable.

Interviewer: I get the impression from what you have said that you are not too confident of the system itself. (Interpretive)

Interviewee: Yes, that's correct. I really don't like it and it is hard for me to defend it with my people. I would really like to talk it over with you and either get a better understanding of it or see if we can change it.

Again, the interview was condensed and made somewhat more simple than some of the day-to-day problems that managers face. However, the technique is a clear-cut one and is often most effective when combined with other methods.

Both the interpretive and reflective methods are a way of seeking information and showing understanding. Another method for showing understanding which may evoke information and can, if not overused, help establish rapport is the supportive response.

Supportive responses

In the supportive response the interviewer or manager shows empathy, agreement, or support for the other person's position. For example, if the interviewee says, "I am quite concerned about costs," the interviewer or boss can be supportive by saying, "Well I can certainly understand your concern and I would like to talk the situation over with you." Another supportive method is to identify with the interviewee. For example, a person new on the job says: "You know, I'm not sure I can handle some of these new methods." The boss may respond supportively by saying, "Well, when I first started in your position I had the same feeling and, in fact, I did have trouble for a while. I can assure you that it will become clear as you go along and we can review it now to try to make it possible for you to move into this new area with confidence."

Listening statements

Listening statements are very similar to the reflective technique. Statements such as "Tell me more," "I understand," or "Please go on" are overt expressions of your desire to listen and to accept the feelings and opinions of the other person even though you may not agree.

Techniques versus Feelings

Some managers and interviewers have difficulty in applying Responsive techniques because they think that by not taking a stand they are somehow compromising their own position. For example, a subordinate says: "I don't like the new policy on overtime." Some managers feel that if one responds by using a reflective response, such as "You are not satisfied with the new system," or by using a listening statement, "Tell me more," that he/she has indicated support or agreement for the subordinate. Therefore, there is a strong temptation to move in and make an assertive statement such as, "The overtime policy is essential under our new government contracts. We must keep these kinds of records and I want you to cooperate."

The fact is that by making a strong Assertive statement the manager may cut off important feedback and leave the subordinate with the feeling that any expression of disagreement or concern is seen as an expression of disloyalty or hostility. Responsive techniques in no way block you from subsequently stating your own position and in every instance you have both the right, and often the responsibility, to clarify your own position before the discussion ends.

In the illustrations which follow, questioning techniques and other Responsive modes are used. You will have an opportunity to judge the impact of these statements as you begin applying them in job situations. The key issue is that genuine responsiveness is an indication of openness, availability, and the capacity to take in new information, to tolerate and respond to conflict and disagreement. It is not an indication of agreement or of relinquishing one's position. In reviewing the use of the Responsive hierarchy, keep in mind that there is no technique that can take the place of a genuine awareness of your own feelings of concern and your genuine readiness to provide others with an opportunity to express their viewpoints and pursue their own goals.

USING THE RESPONSIVE HIERARCHY Given this brief outline of the basic techniques available when one is being Responsive, you can now begin to examine the ways in which you can deal with difficult situations where responsiveness is an appropriate pattern for solving a problem or relating to another person. To clarify the Responsive mode, an illustrative problem will be used and you will be asked to frame responses to that problem.

Here is the problem: You have someone who has worked for you for some time (a subordinate, associate, or someone you know well) to whom you want to talk about performance. That person has not been performing adequately. You and he/she have talked about it several times and on more than one occasion specific goals and objectives have been set. For one reason or another the individual has not been able to meet the goals and as these issues have been discussed he/she indicates something like: "I just don't know what is the matter. I keep trying and I know you have worked with me on this time and time again but I am not sure I have what it takes." After continuing efforts, goal-setting, planning, etc., you have come to the tentative conclusion that it *may* be in the best interests of you and the organization—and perhaps the other person involved—for him/her to be terminated. In any case, you need a clear, definite resolution of the individual's performance problems.

The next step in the process is to move into the Responsive hierarchy and to design responses for each of the major modes suggested in the hierarchy. First, you will be asked to design responses which seek information or show understanding. Next, responses which indicate a willingness to modify or change your own behavior will be shown. In each category an example or comparative response will be given. Check to see if your response contains elements of the comparative answer provided.

Responses designed to seek information Design several responses indicating a desire to obtain information. In order to set the situation a little more clearly, assume that the subordinate (or other individual) has just said: "I know that you want to talk to me today about my performance. I am aware that I have not improved much in the last couple of months." Now design *seeking-information* responses.

1. First, try a direct question.

_____

_____

_____

_____

_____

_____

2. Next, try a discussion or overhead question.

_____

_____

_____

_____

_____

_____

Comparative responses

1. "Do you feel you have gotten sufficient help from me to handle the goals and problems we have talked about?" (Direct question)
2. "Tell me a little bit about what has been going wrong and how you feel about it." (Discussion or overhead question)

Responses designed to show understanding

Now design a response to show understanding. Note again the subordinate has just said, "I know that you want to talk to me today about my performance. I am aware that I haven't improved much in the last couple of months."

1. Design a reflective response to that statement. (Recall that a reflective response includes no judgments or new information, but simply mirrors back or reflects what the other individual has said.)

    Reflective response:_____

    _____

    _____

    _____

    _____

2. Now design an interpretive response:_____

_____

_____

_____

_____

_____

3. Now design a supportive response:_____

_____

_____

_____

_____

_____

Comparative responses

1. "You don't feel you have improved?" (Imply or actually say "tell me more." Reflective response.)

2. "It sounds to me as though you have begun to take it for granted that you are not going to be able to meet goals and you see little likelihood of a change." (Interpretive response)

   Note that interpretive responses show understanding only if they accurately reflect that you understand the other person's point of view rather than becoming pointed or negative. For example, one interpretive response would be to say, "It seems clear to me that you have given up and that you are basically lazy and unconcerned." Here the individual is interpreting but also loading the statement with value judgments and hostility. Thus, an interpretive statement can be Aggressive rather than Responsive and concerned.

3. "Yes, I think I know how you feel. Things have not been going well. I know what it's like when you just cannot seem to make progress." (Supportive response)

Modifying behavior

The next level of the hierarchy is modifying your behavior (or showing a willingness to modify it). Chances are you will find this response a little difficult in a case in which the individual may be close to termination. However, it is possible to show a willingness to modify your behavior even in a difficult situation.

1. For experimental purposes, then, design a response that shows a willingness to modify your behavior without denying your rights or needs or putting yourself down. A response of this type indicates willingness to be influenced by the other, to consider alternatives, to negotiate.

Modifying behavior (yours) response:_____

_____

_____

_____

_____

_____

Comparative response

1. "Well, you're right. I do want to talk to you about your performance, and as things stand now I don't see much opportunity for us to work out another set of goals. Before settling on a course of action, I want to get more information from you. Perhaps there are some alternatives I am unaware of." (Modifying-behavior response)

Changing behavior

As you move toward providing the other person with everincreasing influence you may, particularly when faced with new information, choose to change your behavior. As you begin thinking through the problem, you may become aware of alternatives that had not occurred to you earlier.

Once again, assume your subordinate says, "I know that you want to talk to me today about my performance. I am aware that I haven't improved much in the last couple of months." Assume also that, as you think through the problem, you decide you wish to change your approach from a hard stance to a problem-solving one.

1. Design a response that shows a willingness to change your own behavior. (Be sure the response does not put you in a position that you cannot support personally or organizationally.)

_____

_____

_____

_____

_____

_____

Comparative response

1. "I am concerned about how things have been going. My first feeling as I began reviewing your recent performance was that probably the best thing for you and the company was for you to begin looking for another job. But I am ready to change my position. I believe we can work out some intermediate steps where we can both be satisfied that either performance will be O.K. or that some other action will be taken." (Changing-behavior response)

REVIEWING THE GUIDELINES

Now that the basic techniques of responsiveness have been reviewed, they can be tied in with the responsiveness guidelines outlined earlier. The use of the hierarcy has already been described. The remaining elements include the following:

Tune in to the feelings of others. The basic responsive techniques make it possible to accomplish the two essential steps that must be taken if you want to understand and respond to others. First, you need to find out where the other person stands. If you want to know how someone feels or what he/she thinks, then ask that person. If you encounter resistance, then use some of the less direct techniques like overhead questions or reflective responses.

The second essential step is to seek understanding of the viewpoints of the interviewee. Again, reflective techniques are a useful method for becoming more aware of the feelings and attitudes of others. A somewhat more formal method to ensure that you comprehend is to repeat back to the individual your understanding of his/her position and check for agreement. An example follows: (In this instance assume you are the subordinate trying to understand your boss's point of view.)

Manager: I don't think you're spending enough time with your people. They seem to be out of control and very casual about things. I'm upset by the fact they don't come in on time and they never seem to respond to emergency situations.

Subordinate: I understand that you want my people to respond to emergencies and be on time and meet other job requirements. You would like to see me spend more time with them in giving directions or setting goals. Have I fully understood you?

As indicated earlier, the subordinate has not necessarily indicated that he/she agrees with the boss's criticisms or feelings. Rather he/she is simply checking for understanding. If the boss agrees, then the subordinate may wish to make an Assertive statement regarding his/her own opinion or explore alternatives for dealing with the situation.

Use goal-oriented responses. As is the case in applying assertiveness guidelines, it is important in using questions and other Responsive techniques to direct your attention toward results, goals, and objectives. For example, if two people are having trouble solving a problem you can direct your attention to the relationship: "What is it about her you don't like?" A more positive, goal-oriented statement or question would go something like this: "Well, what do you and she need to do in order to work together to get the results that I'm sure you both want?"

A great many interpersonal tensions and political conflicts can be resolved by seeking out information regarding departmental and organizational goals rather than probing for feelings. This does not mean that exploration of personal feelings and attitudes is undesirable but rather that a preoccupation with the politics or social components of a situation may stand in the way of focusing on key issues. Often personal conflicts are simply a result of a lack of clarity as to function, tasks, or goals.

Clarify and summarize. One of the most useful roles that a counselor or manager can fulfill in working with individuals and groups is to be Responsive to what has happened, rather than simply forcing what he/she wants to have happen. Basically, techniques of clarification and summary are very similar to the reflective approach. In a complex or highly charged situation it is often useful to pull together the feelings and facts that have already been expressed rather than pushing forward with new goals and new issues. A useful and basic ground rule for dealing with difficult situations is: when in doubt, listen, then clarify or summarize.

The advantages of timely summaries are:

1. First, by clarifying and summarizing you are able to get your own thoughts in order.

2. Next, you are able to demonstrate that you do understand and have taken in what's been said or have cleared up any misinterpretations.

3. Finally, you are able to contribute to the other person's awareness of what has been happening.

Avoid self-putdowns.   For many people a basic motivation for using the Responsive mode is to win friends. Rather than using Responsive techniques to learn more about the situation or to aid others in clarifying their own ideas, many managers use these methods to win affection, to appear nice, or to avoid conflict. There is no need to diminish yourself in order to get information, to show understanding, or to offer support. Here are contrasting examples showing sound Responsive statements (or questions) and then inappropriate, apologetic, Nonassertive reactions.

Responsive	*Nonassertive*
Tell me more. (Listening statement)	I'm a little slow. Would you do me a favor and summarize your idea.
What happened? (Overhead question)	Sorry to bother you. I am not pressuring you but I would like to know what happened.
I understand your concern with costs. I share your desire to improve the situation. (Supportive response)	Look, don't worry too much about the cost problem. I have been through this. I'm sure the problem will pass.

When Responsive modes of behavior are aimed at getting information and understanding others, and lead toward genuine problem-solving, there is no need for apologies or self-putdowns.

Integrate content and style.   When your purpose is to draw out and take in information and to open yourself to the influence of others, your message is consistent with your behavior. Here are some of the specific behaviors associated with the Responsive mode:

1. Active listening behavior.

    Active listening involves a *message* that asks for information or feelings and a style that demonstrates a willingness to listen: waiting for the other to respond, maintaining eye contact, framing questions which encourage elaboration, using techniques (reflective, interpretive, supportive) that demonstrate interest and understanding.

2. Avoiding "loaded" questions.

    Asking questions in order to trap or lead the other person in a predetermined direction is *not* a genuine listening response.

Loaded Question (avoid)	*Open Question* (O.K.)
Don't you think you should try to be on time?	What has been causing your lateness?
Why don't you try to make as many sales calls as our more successful sales representatives?	How many calls a day are you making? or How many calls a day do you feel you need to make to reach your sales quota?

3. Modulating tone of voice.

    Responsive behavior is open, interested, inquiring; it does not include whining, tentative, or apologetic inflections, nor an acrimonious, testy tone. Avoid "poor me" delivery. Avoid an Aggressive edge.

4. Using open-ended responses.

    Yes or No questions, leading questions, entrapment, or cross-examination (DA) questions tend to cut down the length and freedom of the respondent's comments. Overhead questions, brief listening statements, and clarifying questions keep the interaction open. Examples:

Avoid	*Use*
Would you like more responsibility? (Yes/No. This cuts off discussion.)	How do you feel about having increased responsibility? (Overhead question. This encourages elaboration.)
Don't you think you would enjoy a new assignment? (Leading question. It cuts down freedom of response.)	Tell me more about how you see your present assignment and what you want in the future. (Listening statement. It encourages elaboration and provides freedom.)
If it bothers you, as you say it has, why have you been over-budget so	As I understand our discussion so far, you're concerned about meet-

often? (Cross-examination or DA question. This creates defensiveness and reduces openness.) ing the budget. (Summary/clarification statement. This encourages elaboration.)

5. Watching gestures, tempo of delivery, other nonverbal behavior.

When you are truly listening you don't rush your questions; you are silent to permit the other to think and answer. You don't dominate the interaction by walking around, waving your arms, or showing impatience. Your physical behavior communicates: "I'm listening, I'll take the time to understand, I'm not simply waiting until you finish to make my point."

PRACTICE Chapters 6 and 7 outlined the Assertive and Responsive behaviors and set forth specific behavior associated with each of these modes. In the next chapter you will have a chance to apply these techniques to selected managerial and leadership situations.

NOTES . 1. C. Rogers, *Counseling and Psychotherapy: Newer Concepts in Practice*, Boston: Houghton Mifflin, 1942.

2. See "Interviewing for Results," © Educational Systems and Designs, Inc., Westport, Connecticut, 1968. See also, "Management Development Program—Preconference Material," © Educational Systems and Designs, Inc., Westport, Conn., 1978.

8

Becoming More Assertive and Responsive. Application and Practice

BEHAVIOR MODELS

Assertive-Responsive (A-R) skills can be practiced and applied by setting up a desirable framework or sequence of events which, if used with individuality and creativity, will move you toward increased effectiveness. As is true in the development of any skill, it is necessary to establish structures, procedures, and ground rules for action as a way of developing desired competency. These frameworks provide models which can be practiced, modified, and expanded upon as you become more comfortable with the procedure and begin drawing upon your own unique resources.

There are two levels of activity involved in applying Assertive and Responsive skills.

1. General procedures.

   First, you need to organize and practice the total repertoire of skills available to you as you interact with others.

2. Application procedures.

   Second, the generalized knowledge and skill associated with Assertive-Responsive behavior must be applied to the achievement of specific goals. For example, Responsive techniques such as questioning, reflecting, and summarizing must be applied to specific leadership situations such as delegating, reviewing performance, and resolving conflict. It is not possible to practice any skill as it applies to every potential leadership problem. However, by improving your capacity to apply your general knowledge and skill to specific situations you can also increase your ability to apply Assertive-Responsive techniques in new or related situations. So if you know how to clarify goals when delegating work, you can apply this same capacity in counseling, reviewing performance, and resolving conflict. In the section that follows you will have an opportunity to review a broad repertoire of Assertive-Responsive techniques and then try them out in specific leadership situations.

BUILDING ASSERTIVE- RESPONSIVE MODELS—THE REPERTOIRE

The concepts, strategies, and techniques associated with Assertive and Responsive behavior can be applied in a wide range of leadership and management situations. Two generalized models—broad frames of reference established for study and application of Assertive-Responsive behavior—are reviewed and summarized below:

To become more Assertive	*To become more Responsive*
1. Use the Assertiveness hierarchy:	1. Use the Responsiveness hierarchy:
a) Give information,	a) Seek information,
b) Express wants,	b) Show understanding,
c) Persuade,	c) Modify behavior,
d) Control.	d) Change behavior.
2. Be expressive.	2. Tune into others' feelings.
3. Be goal oriented.	3. Use goal-oriented responses.

4. Be clear.	4. Clarify and summarize others' points of view.
5. Avoid putdowns.	5. Avoid self-putdowns.
6. Integrate Assertive content and style.	6. Integrate Responsive content and style.

These two how-to models have been described and practiced in earlier chapters. The next step is to apply them to specific leadership functions.

A–R Models— Application

In order to move from the general to the specific it is necessary to select day-to-day leadership concerns to work on. The application exercises that follow involve three steps.

First, two specific leadership functions have been selected so that you can explore and test out how A–R approaches can be applied. These two functions—setting goals and reviewing performance—are basic to leadership and with variations can be applied to many other situations.

Second, each of these functions has been described in a step-by-step format.

Third, illustrations of each step using A–R methods are provided and accompanied by a trial, or practice, exercise.

TWO LEADERSHIP FUNCTIONS

Two of the most critical functions of a leader in any organizational or group setting are (1) establishing direction through setting goals, and (2) reviewing performance in order to maintain and improve results. Two models for applying Assertive-Responsive skills to these functions are provided.

MODEL I. *Setting Goals with Subordinates*

MODEL II. *Reviewing Performance*

Each step required to apply these models will be described and then clarified through a practice problem or example. Clearly, every leader in one way or another plays a role in setting goals, and every leader in one way or another tries to keep people functioning well (formally or informally performance is reviewed). Step-by-step models are not *the* way to behave in each of these areas but they provide an appropriate way to practice your skills systematically. They deal with the core of the management process: establishing and maintaining direction.

MODEL I. SETTING GOALS WITH SUBORDINATES

Here is a step-by-step procedure for setting goals with a subordinate in a face-to-face planning session. The model leaves room for two-way communication; it encourages the subordinate to become involved in shaping goals and in planning for achievement:

| 1. Describe purpose. | (Why meet?) |
| 2. Check for clarity. | (Does the other understand why he/she is here?) |

3. Identify responsibilities.   (What's his/her job?)

4. Obtain subordinate's goal statement.   (How can responsibility be met?)

5. Discuss until agreement is reached.   (What will be done?)

Steps 1 and 2 of the model are needed only at the outset of an initial discussion in a goal-setting endeavor. Once the procedure is underway, Steps 3, 4, and 5 are repeated for each goal. The process will become clearer as the procedural model is now converted into actual behavior. Here is a script for showing how these five steps might be carried out appropriately. The A–R technique is identified for each step.

1. **Describe purpose** (be Assertive, give information, and express wants).

   Manager: As I mentioned to you when we set up this date, our purpose today would be to identify specific goals that we both feel need to be achieved in order to be sure the department meets overall objectives. We will review your responsibilities one by one—be sure we are in agreement about them—and in each instance develop specific targets for achievement and when and how those achievements will be measured. We will get together periodically to review the goals and if things change we may have to modify the goals and develop new approaches to getting where we want to go.

2. **Check for clarity** (be Responsive and seek information).

   Manager: Do you have any questions about this procedure or any suggestions as to how you feel we can proceed most effectively?

   Subordinate: No. I've taken part in goal-planning sessions before and I think it would be most helpful if we could get some specific targets in some of the areas that are hard to measure.

3. **Identify responsibilities** (be Assertive, give information, and express wants).

   Manager: O.K., let's move on then. One of your major responsibilities —I'm sure we agree this is high priority—is the recruitment, selection, and placement of employees.

4. **Obtain subordinate's goal statement** (be Responsive and seek information).

   Manager: We have agreed in the past that we want no more than one opening at any one time. Right now there are three openings in your department. How do you want to proceed?

   Subordinate: Well, I sure would like to fill those jobs in the next couple of months. However, experience tells me that we are not going to get the kind of applicants we need. We don't have a strong recruitment program. Frankly, I think it would be more realistic to say we will probably get one really appropriate candidate selected and placed in the next 60 days or so and then it will take us another month or two to get the second person. I doubt if we'll have all three positions filled for perhaps six months.

5. **Discuss until agreement is reached.** From this point on, the discussion can be as brief or as long as it needs to be to establish a clear-cut measurable goal and to develop mechanisms for achieving it. The basic pattern of behavior suggested by the general models presented earlier is to move into the Assertive-Responsive mode starting at the lower levels of the hierarchy and working up as needed to achieve desired outcomes. So the continuation of the example shows an exchange of information using Assertive and Responsive modes.

Manager: Well, I gather then that you feel part of the difficulty is that we don't have an effective enough recruitment effort to attract the people we need. (R—showing understanding, and clarifying and summarizing the other person's point of view.)

Subordinate: Yes, I think that's the major problem. There is a genuine shortage of the people we need. That means we have to be more active in reaching out into the job market, establishing relationships in universities, and so on.

Manager: Do you have figures with you, or can we get them, on what we are now spending on recruitment for a year and on what it costs us per person? (R—seeks information.)

Subordinate: Yes, I got those figures together recently and that's one of the things we should talk about. If we include advertising and staff costs as well as travel to meet applicants and so on, we are spending about $28,000 a year for the entire department and we're hiring about six people a year at a little over $4000 per person. I would like to spend more money on recruitment and fill those jobs quickly.

Manager: Well, we might experiment with increasing our expenditures during the next two months and check to see whether that produces more applicants and ultimately more placements. By using this approach we would have a better idea of how we are doing. How do you feel about that kind of an approach? (A–R—Note the manager moves up the hierarchy and uses persuasion: "We'd have a better idea. . . . " Then the manager seeks information.)

Subordinate: That makes a lot of sense to me. At least we would have a better idea of the cost-effectiveness of our recruitment dollars and it might also give us a better indication of how tight the job market is. I would like to establish an increased recruitment expenditure and plan on hiring two new people in the next two months.

The manager and subordinate continue interacting in order to pin down what can be accomplished and when. They may establish checkpoints and discuss "how" in more detail. Basically, however, at this point a direction has been set and a basis for agreement is established.

Thus, the basic model for setting goals provides the procedural format for goal setting; the models for Assertive and Responsive behavior provide specific techniques, such as giving information in an affirmative way, seeking the opinions of others, showing concern with both content and feelings, and so on. The next step in the process is for you to try out a goal-setting situation.

Setting Goals with Subordinates — Practice

Here is a hypothetical and structured case designed to provide you with an opportunity to practice and check out Assertive-Responsive methods in setting goals.

Case. Developing the subordinate who doesn't develop others.

Assume that you have a subordinate who is responsible for training and developing his/her subordinates. Your subordinate gives directions, and specifies goals, but rarely carries out the responsibility to review performance or engage people in training programs or development activities. You feel he/she should be reviewing performance, counseling subordinates, and setting up development plans. You want to set goals for your subordinate to develop others. The five-step behavioral model is repeated below and you are asked to apply the model.

1. Describe purpose.
2. Check for clarity.
3. Identify responsibilities.
4. Obtain subordinate's goal statements.
5. Discuss until agreement is reached.

Step 1. Describe purpose

Practice exercise. Here are three statements of purpose. Comment on how you feel about each statement. Was it assertive? If not, why not? First, read all three statements, then check one as best. Finally, read the comparative analysis.

1. _____

1. *Manager:* Your job is to build our organization. You're not getting the results you should be getting so I want to go over your responsibilities and clear up any weak spots. If we can't get this place running smoothly, then the department is going to be in trouble.

Comment:_____

_____

_____

_____

_____

_____

_____

2. _____   2. *Manager:* Top management wants me to review your performance. The first step is to check your responsibilities; I will see if you are meeting them and will set goals to straighten out any problems.

Comment:_____

_____

_____

_____

_____

_____

3. _____   3. *Manager:* My purpose today is to discuss your responsibilities and to reach agreement on goals which will continue moving your department forward.

Comment:_____

_____

_____

_____

_____

_____

Here you will find a comparative analysis of each of the statements to aid you in assessing your own answer and in thinking through your own goals and feelings regarding the application of this first step of the model.

Comparative analysis. Both Statements 1 and 2 had, to some extent, a negative quality. Rather than using positive and affirmative statements the manager used words like "trouble," "straighten out," "weak spots," "problems" and there were some putdowns. There were quite a few value judgments involved rather than straight information, expressions of affirmative feelings, and efforts to develop a climate to encourage open, two-way communication. Statement 1 was dogmatic. Negative consequences were pointed out before any information had been shared. Statement 2 was formal and negative. In statement 3 there was a brief, clear presentation of purpose and an optimistic approach using the idea of moving forward.

Step 2. Check for clarity

Practice exercise. In the space provided below, indicate what you would say *after* identifying your purpose. How would you check for understanding? Write a brief Responsive statement, then look over the comparative analysis.

_____

_____

_____

_____

_____

_____

_____

Comparative analysis. Checking for clarity involves asking a question or in one way or another indicating a desire to be sure the other person understands. Questions like, Is that clear? Do you have any suggestions? How does that sound to you? all provide the subordinate with an opportunity to respond and express his/her viewpoint.

Step 3. Identify responsibility

Practice exercise. In the space below, write out a brief statement of your subordinate's responsibility regarding training and development. Assume your subordinate has been charged with developing people and keeping them informed as to how they can improve.

Statement:_____

_____

_____

_____

_____

_____

Now refer to the checklist that follows to aid you in evaluating your statement.

Checklist

An overall list of components present in Assertive-Responsive statements was provided at the beginning of the chapter. A more detailed description of how to come across assertively and responsively was outlined earlier. The following checklist focuses on some of the key points to be considered within this general framework.

If your statement of responsibility (above) was Assertive and took into consideration that this is a relatively early stage of the discussion, it will meet the criteria below. (Check those statements that apply.)

_____ I emphasized giving information and identifying responsibility rather than persuading, controlling, or pointing out negative consequences. (The lower levels of the Assertive hierarchy were used in order to get started in an open, easy fashion.)

_____ I used positive affirmative language.

Rather than saying there is a "problem" or we need to "straighten out your job," etc., the statement should sound more like "developing subordinates is one of your key responsibilities."

_____ My statements were clear.

Even though this is a hypothetical situation, the chances are that as a manager you might feel some tension or hostility toward a subordinate who evidently has not been developing his/her people. It is important, therefore, to be aware of the fact that you have a feeling about this and then to convert that feeling into a positive, affirmative act. Statements like "I feel strongly," or, "I am extremely interested in" are indications of your true feelings _without_ a negative connotation, that is, "Things are going wrong," "I am not happy with," etc.

_____ My statements were purposeful (goal-oriented).

Since this is a business and goal-oriented discussion and since you presumably feel positively about it, the words and general nature of your delivery should be consistent with this goal-oriented, serious business concern. Casual, capricious comments are inappropriate styles of delivery, as are heavy comments. And so an inappropriate style of delivery would be to make light of the situation. "I know you have a lot of good people out there and you have a lot of things on your mind. It's no big deal but I would like to talk a little today about your responsibility for developing people." This casual, somewhat flip comment and delivery detracts from your presumed genuine concern and assertive posture regarding the development of this area. An inappropriate, heavy approach would go something like: "Well, I just don't know what we're going to do about your failure to carry out one of your basic responsibilities."

And so, based on this checklist and earlier reviews of Assertive behavior, take another look at your own statements and if you feel you can improve or modify them, do so in the space provided below. As you rethink the statements try to think of ways to make them more clear, more concise, and more affirmative.

New statement of responsibility:_____

_____

_____

_____

_____

_____

_____

*Step 4. Obtain
subordinate's
goal statement*

Practice exercise.   Write a statement/question seeking out your subordinate's view:

_____

_____

_____

_____

_____

_____

Comparative analysis: Note that in order to get a clear and open statement from your subordinate, it is essential that you not make your own position so strong that he/she has no room to be creative or Responsive or to express his/her own feelings. If your statement of the goal is something like: "How do you feel about sitting down with each of your subordinates once a month, filling out an appraisal form, and submitting that form to me?" you may have cut off the opportunity for two-way flow of information by being too specific, too soon. When thinking through the fourth step it is important to recognize that in earlier statements you began to set up an attitude, a climate, a mode of interaction that will determine in large measure whether your subordinate feels free to express disagreement or explore his/her true feelings and objectives.

When Steps 1, 2, and 3 have been handled openly and effectively, then Step 4 simply involves saying: "What are your ideas?" or "What do you think?" or "How do you think we should go about this?" or "Do you see other ways in which we might maintain the levels of performance we want?" Statements or questions of this type get the subordinate's point of view out into the open.

*Step 5. Discuss until
agreement is reached*

Practice exercise.   Once the process is underway in an Assertive-Responsive fashion, it can then move into a genuine problem-solving endeavor. In the material that follows, you have an opportunity to try out, in written form, Assertive-Responsive patterns. In each instance the subordinate's statement will be given and you will be asked to design a specific response. The guidelines for developing this response will be outlined in the process. Assume that after some discussion your subordinate seems resistant and says something like the following:

Subordinate: I see my subordinates on a day-to-day basis. We have a lot of meetings together and a formal performance review system is just that. It's a formality and doesn't contribute much to getting the job done.

The first and most important ground rule in any problem-solving endeavor is to stay at the lower levels of the Assertive-Responsive hierarchy rather than escalating into persuasion, disagreement, or attempts to control behavior, and finally either getting into a conflict or creating a situation where your subordinate merely stops interacting and withdraws. Therefore, your statement or response will be at the lower levels of the hierarchy; that is, give information, seek information, avoid sanctions (benefits or negative consequences of what you want), and avoid prematurely knuckling under or changing your own behavior. Assume your subordinate has just said: "I see my people every day. I don't need a formal review system." Now design an Assertive statement in response to your subordinate's comment.

Assertive statement:_____

_____

_____

_____

_____

_____

_____

In assessing your own statement, use the checklist provided and specifically review the following:

_____ My statement was brief.

_____ It avoided putdowns.

_____ It in part reflected my feelings, or provided an opportunity to explore the feelings of the other.

_____ It moved in a goal-oriented direction rather than toward personalities.

If the checklist applies, the chances are that your statement was affirmative and Assertive.

Following are some comparative examples to aid you in assessing your own statement and thinking through ways in which low hierarchy assertions can be applied:

Assertive statement: "Well, I agree that every manager has a lot of opportunities to work with his/her people. As I see it, one of the goals of formalizing any process is to set priorities and to ensure there are no gaps in the system." Or, "I think it's valuable to spend time with your people on a day-to-day basis and I agree there's a lot of contact. I want to explore some of the ways in which that day-to-day contact can be enhanced." Or, "I want to discuss ways in which we can make formal performance review more appropriate and more useful to you and to your subordinates.''

A second alternative in dealing with your subordinate's resistance is to use a Responsive comment. In this second approach you are asked to write out a Responsive reaction to the same issue. In some ways the Responsive comment may be more suitable since the subordinate has taken an opposing position and it is necessary to explore and understand that postion before affirmative action can be taken. You may do that by asking a direct question or by using one or more of the responses covered in the discussion of the Responsive mode. Remember, the subordinate has said something like: "I see my people every day. I don't need a formal performance review."

Responsive comment:_____

_____

_____

_____

_____

_____

_____

Review the Responsive checklist.

_____ I used a reflective or overhead question to seek information and show understanding.

_____ I avoided loaded questions or expressions of hostility.

_____ I sought out feelings.

_____ My goal was to clarify the other's statement rather than win the argument.

Comparative statements: For example, here are some desirable statements. "I see. Tell me more about how your subordinates react to your daily discussion." Or, "You feel the formal system doesn't work?" or, "I understand your reservations. How might we make the system work better?"

Undesirable statements: "Other people make the system work—why can't you?" or, "Have you considered the possibility that you may not be handling the reviews very well?" or, "Why don't you cooperate?"

Goal Setting. Summary   And so the interaction can proceed. By using the models and procedures provided, you have built a two-way exchange leading toward understanding and commitment. In addition, the goal-setting model is appropriate in a wide range of problem-solving situations and is similar to steps used in delegating and assigning work, and in establishing understanding of new procedures.

MODEL II. REVIEWING PERFORMANCE

After goals have been agreed upon, it is necessary to review progress. Is the subordinate meeting the goals on schedule? Are there unanticipated problems? Should the goal be modified due to changing circumstances? Does the subordinate need help, such as training, counseling, other resources? Once again a step-by-step procedure will be provided.

Then you will be asked to try out the procedure using Assertive and Responsive behaviors. Comparative analyses and responses are provided. Clearly, the comparative statements provided are not the only way to respond; nor are they necessarily the best way. They are Assertive or Responsive statements which you can use as a partial check on your own responses.

The Model for Reviewing Performance

1. State purpose.
2. Review specific goal performance.
3. Obtain subordinate's views.
4. Modify or reinforce goals.
5. Review "how-to."
6. Develop commitment.

Scripts showing the model follow. In each case write out your response and then compare it with the script and analysis provided. Review checklists as provided.

Background. Your subordinate has missed an agreed-upon target on cost reduction. Here is a script for discussing this performance goal.

1. State purpose.

   Manager: Fill in Assertive statement (remember to start with the basic purpose of the meeting).

   _____

   _____

   _____

   _____

   _____

   _____

   Comparative statement: "Today I want to go over your key goals. If things have changed we may want to review some of the goals and discuss plans for achievement during the next several meetings." (*Note.* Don't jump immediately into the problem; establish a framework first.)

2. Review specific goal performance (assume cost goals haven't been met, that production and quality goals have been exceeded).

    Manager: (Write out your statement.)_____

    _____

    _____

    _____

    _____

    _____

    _____

Review an assertiveness checklist.

_____ I used positive, affirmative language.

_____ My statement was clear (straightforward and concise).

_____ My statement was goal-oriented (not about personal traits).

_____ I avoided putdowns.

> *Comparative statement:* "You and your staff have put a lot of effort into reaching and exceeding production and quality goals. Your results in those areas are better than we expected when we set them. Costs have gone beyond what we expected and we need to review your goals and determine whether there are ways to make the operation more cost effective. We may need to revise cost goals."

3. Obtain subordinate's view.

    Write out your next response aimed at determining the subordinate's view regarding performance, particularly cost effectiveness.

    _____

    _____

    _____

    _____

    _____

    _____

    _____

> *Comparative analysis:* Overhead or listening statements are usually best early in the discussion. Examples: "How do you see the cost situation?" "Tell me how you feel about your cost goals." "How can we maintain the good operating results you've been getting and improve cost effectiveness?"

4. Modify or reinforce goals.

   Assume the subordinate says: "Actually, my department is more cost effective than we targeted—production has gone up—so even though we are spending more dollars, we have had more output, and that surely makes us more cost effective."

   Write in your response designed to modify or reinforce goal. (Assume costs have gone up at the same rate as production and you feel there should be some increased effectiveness resulting from increased production.)

   _____

   _____

   _____

   _____

   _____

   _____

   _____

   Comparative statement: "We need to establish new goals based on increased production. Increased volume may provide opportunity for savings on unit cost so we need to set new goals reflecting new levels of production." Or, "When production goes up we do realize some reduction in *unit* cost. I think we should set some new goals encompassing the increased *total* cost and the *unit* cost savings."

5. Review "how-to."

   Assume the subordinate needs new and better cost information. Design a how-to statement—an assertion of how he/she should proceed.

   _____

   _____

   _____

   _____

   _____

   _____

   _____

   Comparative statement: "There are several steps you might take. You can refigure unit costs and come up with a new budget; and in addition, you need to consider increasing the work force and the financial effect of a bigger payroll over the next twelve months."

6. Develop commitment.

In making commitments there often needs to be some give and take followed by a summary of the agreement between you and your subordinate. Basically the mode is A–R, something like the following:

Manager: I'd like you to refigure unit costs and then let's set an appropriate goal for the next quarter.

Subordinate: Well, production demands have gone up so fast I didn't have the people to handle the work. I had to schedule overtime and that ran up costs.

Now write your statement to summarize the situation and move toward commitment.

Manager: _____

_____

_____

_____

_____

_____

_____

Comparative analysis: Your statement will be most effective if it shows understanding of the other's position and *then* points to positive action. Here is an example to compare with your statement: "I understand that with a given upsurge in production you would need to schedule some overtime. Therefore, in projecting your costs for the next quarter, figure in enough overtime to carry the operation until you can get more trained people. Your new plan should include what your goals are for training or hiring new people based on production forecasts for the next three or four quarters."

Reviewing Performance — Summary   In the illustration it's apparent that the manager can give feedback, express his/her views, make suggestions, and seek information without putting the other person down or being apologetic. Depending on the amount and nature of resistance, the manager may need to spend more time seeking out the subordinate's opinions, showing understanding, and providing more opportunity for a two-way exchange. Your own approach depends, in part, on your basic style and the nature of your relationships with your subordinates. Nevertheless, the same model still applies. You may choose to spend more time soliciting and responding to your subordinate's views. You can't go wrong if, when in doubt, you take the time to interact and to problem solve in an Assertive-Responsive fashion.

NEXT STEPS   You've had a chance to try out Assertive-Responsive behavior in two hypothetical situations. The most difficult leadership problems occur when you encounter resistance, hostility, or genuine disagreement. Therefore, the next chapter will provide a framework for using Assertive-Responsive skills and behavior in dealing with conflict.

9

Becoming More Assertive and Responsive. Conflict Resolution

CONFLICT RESOLUTION STRATEGIES

In several previous sections a key point has been made; that is, aggression, anger, competitiveness are a part of organizational life. These feelings, relationships, and reactions are normal and inescapable. They can escalate into unresolved conflict, they can create personal tensions and organizational trauma. Unresolved and inappropriate conflict has caused businesses to fail and individuals to flounder; it can eat away at human resources just as much as the technical, physical, and natural resources that are essential to sustaining organizational life. Therefore, increased skill in resolving conflict is as basic to organizational success as is the ability to handle the day-to-day managerial and organizational affairs most typically associated with the management and leadership role.

The Leadership Model describes basic modes of reacting and responding which can be translated into conflict resolution modes or strategies.

Aggression

Aggression is most often a device for staying on top, a device for winning and not admitting to one's own deficiencies. The nature of Aggressive behavior precludes open communication and two-way problem solving. Essentially, it is a way of suppressing conflict, of avoiding it by being one-up. At times it is a way of defending oneself or of shocking the other person into awareness of one's rights. Often it creates resistance and escalates conflict to higher levels of intensity.

Nonassertiveness

The Nonassertive mode is used to escape conflict or to be so accommodating and harmonizing that conflict never crops up. The absence of conflict in a personal or organizational situation is usually an indication that people are not pursuing goals, personal feelings, and ambitions in a forceful and straightforward fashion. Nonassertive behavior is manifest when one is refraining from utilizing or applying his/her true feelings or resources, or when one is engaged in gameplaying or manipulations in order to avoid conflict or to escape criticism or attack.

Assertive Behavior

When you give information, persuade, sell, or even point up negative consequences, you are dealing with conflict by pushing assertively for results and desired outcomes. When you are engaged in efforts to resolve differences and develop commitment among peers, associates, managers, and subordinates, then giving information, persuading, and selling is often an inadequate strategy and, at best, incomplete. It does not seek out the cause of the conflict; it does not draw upon or show overt interest in opposing viewpoints and the resources of others. The strategy is appropriate in order to make your position clear as an input to two-way influence. It is also useful when most resistance has been overcome and one is striving to close on the issue, or when resistance is low and the other person is open and available to influence.

Responsive Behavior   Seeking out the opinions of others, and being Responsive and open to them is a necessary ingredient in conflict resolution. If, however, you do not assert yourself, if you do not act on your knowledge and feelings, you may end up with an outcome that is not optimum or that violates your rights.

Assertive-Responsive Behavior   This is the most appropriate conflict resolution response because it involves the resources of both of the parties involved. Thus, in a union–management conflict it is essential for management to know what the union wants, where it stands, and what it is after. Conversely, the union must have that same kind of information about management. Thus each of the parties must, in some way and at some point, assert a position, put out information, and perhaps engage in selling or convincing others as to the rectitude of their stance. Conversely, each of the parties—if the conflict is to be surfaced and resolved—must be willing to listen, to draw out, and to be Responsive and open to the views of others. Responsiveness does not deny the capacity of one to argue or take a strong position. In the Assertive-Responsive mode, conflict resolution occurs because both parties are willing to take a stand while at the same time both are willing to listen to the other. Although things may get tight or tough and although arguments may occur, as long as both parties continue to clarify their own positions and seek out understanding of the other, there is the potential that common ground will be found and a mutual goal can be developed. The reality is that union–management conflicts do get resolved in the large majority of cases without strikes and without disruptive attacks. This is also true of interpersonal affairs. Husbands and wives may fight a great deal but they find ways of raising children and solving daily problems, and they spend a great deal of their time in collaborative effort. Managers and subordinates, peers, and competitive departments may frequently argue and may have different short-term goals and objectives. Successful organizations find ways of resolving conflict and developing courses of action which are in the best interests of the organization and its members.

USING THE HIERARCHIES

Certainly, in any interpersonal or organizational situation there are times when people do not behave in accordance with any idealized set of ground rules. People lose their tempers, and they sometimes manipulate and play games. At times they spend more time selling than listening, and at times they try to satisfy others rather than be clear about what they want or what is genuinely best from their point of view. However, many of these obstacles to conflict resolution can be removed or reduced through the utilization of the techniques outlined in the Assertive-Responsive hierarchies. There is a sequence of levels of response for appropriately utilizing the Assertive-Responsive hierarchy in resolving conflict.

Level 1:   In resolving conflict it is often best to be Responsive before becoming Assertive and to stay at the lower levels of the hierarchy. (Be R first, that is, seek information and show understanding.)

Level 2: As the conflict resolution continues, one strives to move toward an Assertive-Responsive pattern where one both gives and receives information, and to stay at lower levels of the hierarchy. (Be A–R next; give and seek information, express your wants, and show understanding for the goals of the other.)

Level 3: If the problem-solving process isn't working, one can then choose to escalate the process by being Assertive without including a Responsive component. (Be A; take a firm position as appropriate.)

If this Level 3 approach fails, or if the initial attack is highly personal or destructive, then there are two additional options:

a) Escalate further whereby you become increasingly Assertive (move up the hierarchy by pointing out benefits of your position, or escalate further by pointing out negative consequences) or in survival situations move into Aggressive behavior. (Be A; be persuasive or controlling.)

b) Try moving back to the earlier level of the process, that is, become increasingly Responsive. (Be R.)

This process seems complicated at first but becomes quite clear as one observes it in practice. In the script that follows, Mr. or Ms. A is the *aggressor* and Mr. or Ms. B is using conflict resolution strategies.

Level 1   *Mr(s). A.:* I don't like the way things have been going and I don't feel you are being fair. You're playing politics at my expense. I thought I could trust you but if that is the game you're playing I am going to find ways of getting even.

Mr(s). B, as the supervisor or peer, has a variety of choices to make. He/she probably feels attacked. He/she can escalate the conflict by attacking back, or he/she can move into the Nonassertive mode and be apologetic and seek the support and affection of his/her subordinate. A third alternative is that he/she can simply assert his/her own position. The suggestion, however, in the proposed approach is that it is usually better at the early stages of disagreement to be Responsive, to show interest and concern and a willingness to listen in order to open up the process. Therefore, a sample recommended Level 1 response is the following:

Mr(s). B: Well, I can see you are angry and upset. I want to understand what it is that's bothering you. Tell me more. (R)

You will note that the emphasis in this response is on hearing, on listening. At the same time there is no apology, no self-denigration, and no attack. Assume the conversation continues as follows:

Mr(s). A: Look, I've heard that before. You're always interested and concerned but you never do anything about it. I thought I could rely on your support and could trust you but it doesn't look that way.

Once again, the manager or respondent can choose to escalate the situation, to become Aggressive, put the other person down, etc. He or she can become Nonassertive or apologetic, or can at this point assert his/her own position. Again, for purposes of the illustration, the Level 1 responsive mode will be used before introducing an Assertive component. So the manager, Mr(s). B, might say:

Mr(s). B: (Option 1) Tell me specifically, what's been happening? (R—overhead question.)

Note that there is a wide range of options available at this Responsive level, including the various techniques that have been illustrated earlier. To further illustrate and clarify them, here are some additional Responsive comments that might be used at this juncture.

Mr(s). B: (Option 2) You are angry at me for something that has been going wrong. (R—interpretive.)

Mr(s). B: (Option 3) Look, I can see you are angry and I know how I feel when people don't respond the way I expect them to. I really want to understand specifically what it is you are angry about. (R—supportive.)

In each of the options the manager is not closing off communication; he/she is not putting the person down. His/her questions or statements may create some tension or friction but there is, nevertheless, a demonstrated willingness to hear, to listen, and to take in information.

It is important to recognize that very often when people are angry they want to argue. Asking the other person to listen or appealing to logic or asking him/her to calm down may be the exact opposite of what will help solve the problem. Taking in and being aware of someone else's anger is a first step in showing respect and concern for that person, even though at some point you may want to make it clear that you have your own self-interest and self-respect to consider also.

Some exceptions There are times when listening or tuning in to others may seem like weakness and may be an inadequate mode for defending oneself. For example, assume an associate (boss, subordinate, peer) loses his or her temper and says to you:

"I think you're a miserable S.O.B."

None of the Responsive modes seems quite right: "Tell me more" or "Why do you feel that way?" aren't sufficiently strong or self-protective. Therefore, at times one may feel that a problem-solving attitude or response is simply not an adequate emotional reaction. It follows that you may choose to become highly Assertive or Aggressive if you are personally or severely attacked. The limitation of Aggressive behavior is that it can quickly escalate and get out of control. Therefore, using your own feelings and experience, it is often best to lessen the tensions in a conflict situation by being Responsive. And so the first suggested response to conflict, in general, is to be Responsive, without giving up your rights or denying your resources. You are thereby still in a position to escalate, to move to the next higher, Assertive level of conflict resolution: Level 2.

Level 2   The second level of conflict resolution is to combine assertiveness and responsiveness. It is probable that in some situations it may be appropriate to begin at the second level. That is, if the situation is not highly charged, or conversely, if you feel a need to make your position clear immediately, then the Assertive-Responsive mode may be appropriate. Keep in mind, however, that often by being Responsive first you gain more information and then your Assertive statement will make more sense and have more impact. Assume, therefore, in this instance that the subordinate continues his/her attack and you choose to move to the Assertive-Responsive mode (A-R).

Mr(s). A: Look, I've told you about this before. I am just totally dissatisfied with the kind of support I've been getting from you and from the rest of management. I am out on a limb and nobody gives me any help. You people just cannot be relied on.

Mr(s). B: I can see that something is going on out there that is really bothering you but we can't solve the problem unless I know what happened. (A-R— First the manager summarized and interpreted responsively, and then made an assertion.)

Or, another option for Mr(s). B: "You've been putting me down for the last five minutes. I feel strongly that your attack is unjustified and that I have been dealing with you and your department frankly and openly. If there are specific problems that are unresolved then let's get to those problems. What are the issues?" (A-R—gives information, indicates his/her feelings, and asks a question.)

Level 3   If the individual persists, then it may be appropriate to take the strong Assertive stance without a Responsive component; something like this:

I want you to stop name-calling. If you don't stick with the issues we're not going to get to the bottom of this. (A)

Or, another strong assertion:

Unless you are willing to return to the issues I am going to end this conversation. (A)

Or,

I want you to submit a specific list of your concerns and back them up with evidence. (A)

Conflict Resolution   This basic model for dealing with conflict can be enhanced and expanded by integrating it with the earlier hierarchies that were mentioned. You will recall that in being Responsive the least compromising and most open approaches were at the lower end of the hierarchy. Thus, at the start of a conflict situation it is better to seek information or show understanding than to immediately modify your behavior or show a willingness to change. If every time you are confronted by conflict or aggression you immediately show a willingness to back off or modify, clearly you begin to compromise your own strength and self-respect as well as present a wishy-washy image to those with whom you work. Similarly, the most appropriate Assertive responses early in the conflict situation are those at the lower end of the scale. That is, it is better to give information and express a want than it is to begin selling or pointing out negative consequences right at the start of a conflict situation. A manager can respond with these techniques, keeping the conflict at a low level and at the same time not backing down or putting him/herself down in the process.

Here are some additional examples of various levels of conflict resolution responses:

Example 1 *Mr(s). A:* (a peer or subordinate) You know, I'm really angry about department B. They are supposed to work with us. They haven't been cooperative and I don't feel that you have done very much to help me in getting them straightened out.

Mr(s). B: Well, I can see you are upset and I want to understand exactly what's been happening. Tell me more. (R: Shows understanding, reflects awareness of other's feelings.)

Example 2 *Mr(s). A:* Well, the main thing that I'm griping about is they seem to be able to get away with all kinds of shortcuts and my group is always getting criticized when things go wrong you never back us up. I don't think you're in tune with what we are up against.

Mr(s). B: I feel confident that I understand your goals and some of the obstacles you face (give information). Tell me more of what you mean about being supportive and backing you up (seek information). (A–R)

Note that both of those responses are at the lower levels of the hierarchies. In contrast, note an alternative where one immediately moves to higher levels.

"If you continue to accuse me of being uninformed without giving me any information, then you can't expect that I am going to give you much help." (A—pointing out negative consequences.) "When I truly understand the situation I am sure I can make the changes needed so that we can get the results we want." (R—showing a willingness to change behavior.)

Clearly, at this early stage of the conflict it doesn't make much sense on the one hand to start pointing out negative consequences and cutting the conversation off, nor does it make much sense to show a premature willingness to change before the facts are collected.

Practice In order to clarify and practice the ways in which the conflict resolution strategies apply in work situations, here are a few examples.

A subordinate comes to you and is very upset because he/she did not receive an increase which he/she expected. He/she says: "I feel I am being treated unfairly."

Design a Responsive statement or question for that subordinate. Make it at the lower end of the responsiveness hierarchy. (Seek information or show understanding—R.)

_____

_____

_____

_____

_____

_____

_____

Next, assume that the subordinate says, "Look, I think you have the facts. You know that I deserve an increase and I'm sure that there are politics at work here. I have been bypassed in favor of someone who is closer to the people at the top."

Design an Assertive-Responsive comment. Keep it at the lower levels of Assertive-Responsive behavior. That is, give information, express a want, and seek information or show understanding. (A–R)

_____

_____

_____

_____

_____

_____

_____

Again, assume the conflict continues and you decide to escalate into an Assertive statement without a Responsive component. The subordinate says: "Look, I have heard that kind of thing before and everybody talks a nice game, but when the chips are down, it's the politicians who get paid off. I have been doing a good job and I don't see why I am not compensated for it."

Design a strongly Assertive statement (pointing out positive benefits or negative consequences) without a Responsive component. (A)

_____

_____

_____

_____

_____

_____

Assume that the individual continues to argue and that you decide, rather than escalating further, to try once again to draw him/her out through the Responsive mode.

Design a Responsive statement you feel might open up the conversation further. Design that response assuming that the subordinate has just said: "We've talked about this now for ten or fifteen minutes and you haven't given me one fact to convince me that I am wrong. You know that Sam Jones got an increase and it just seems to me that the only way he could get one instead of me is because somebody upstairs likes him. The system is unfair and as far as I can see you are a party to that system."

Design a response (R).

_____

_____

_____

_____

_____

_____

Response Techniques   In order to provide some contrasting responses, here is the same situation with a variety of response techniques used to de-escalate the conflict and move toward problem solving.

Subordinate: I thought I was going to get an increase. I didn't get it and I think that's unfair. It's a political system. It doesn't matter what you do, it's who you know.

Manager: I can see you're angry and upset but I'm not sure what happened to make you think things are political. Tell me more about it. (R—question and reflection.)

Subordinate: Look, I've been here long enough to know that the people who know the right people are the ones who get a raise and you know I didn't get a raise. I just feel that I haven't been treated fairly and that you haven't leveled with me.

Manager: You feel that in some way or other I have not been straight or clear with you? (R—reflective response. Implicit request for the individual to give more information.)

Subordinate: You're quite right. When we talked a couple of months ago it seemed to me that you were saying I was doing a good job but then you didn't live up to your promises.

Manager: Last time we spoke about this I told you you were doing a good job. The first thing I want to be clear about is that you were not promised an increase. So if there is something that happened that made you think a promise was made or that other people were given some kind of an advantage, I'd like to know more about it. (A–R—an assertion followed by a Responsive inquiry is used to clarify the situation and at the same time attempt to keep it at a problem-solving level.)

Subordinate: Well, the fact is that Sam Jones got an increase and as far as I can see the only reason he got one is that he knows some people upstairs.

Manager: Well, I don't think it's useful or appropriate for me to talk about Sam Jones. Let's look specifically at your performance and the possibilities and requirements involved in your getting an increase. (A—gives information, expresses goals.)

Assume however, that the subordinate continues to escalate the conflict.

Subordinate: Well, you say we shouldn't talk about Sam Jones but the fact is that it's because he is a politician that he got ahead of me. I think that's unfair. You didn't have anything to do with promoting him but you are part of the system.

At this point the manager may decide to use an escalated assertion and at the same time maintain the possibility of problem solving by finishing with an indication that he/she is willing to modify his/her behavior, that is, be Responsive.

Manager: If you continue complaining about the past rather than trying to work through a solution for the future, we will never get to a discussion of where you stand, why you haven't received an increase so far, and what you need to do to get one in the future. If your desire is to determine how to get ahead, then focus on that issue or you are going to lose out. Tell me more about your goals and how you plan to get results. (A–R)

Note at this point the subordinate may continue to ventilate some of his feelings but may recognize that it is more appropriate to move in a new direction. Consequently, he might say something like the following:

Subordinate: Well, I still think the system has been unfair in the past but I guess there's no point in pushing it. I just feel I ought to get an increase and that's what I want to talk about.

Now the manager has a chance to return to the problem-solving process but also at the appropriate time to clarify his/her own feelings about what has been going on. To abbreviate the conversation somewhat, some of the manager's responses will be combined in this next brief example as he/she answers.

Manager: OK, fine, let's talk about your future. I want to be very specific about your goals and responsibilities and your performance against those goals and responsibilities. I also want to make it clear that much of what you've said about me and the politics of this organization are not accurate and I want to clear that up. First, let's get specific about the results you've been getting and how you can go about improving them.

Conflict and Tension

The process which has just been described outlines ways in which conflict can be escalated and de-escalated. The model is built upon the psychological premise that when there is too much tension in a given system, the system does not function effectively. Thus, if a boss and a subordinate are both angry, disturbed, and busily engaged in putting each other down, there is little chance that, while that excess of tension is present, problems will be solved or relationships improved. Thus, one of the ways of improving any relationship or system is to reduce excessive tension. The levels of escalation and de-escalation suggest that the best way to reduce the tension in a system is to acknowledge and respond to that tension. In interpersonal affairs this means providing others with an opportunity to express their feelings, their anger, their dissatisfaction (without denying one's own rights, resources, or capacity to defend oneself). In organizational affairs this same kind of conflict-resolution strategy is appropriate. Coaching and counseling, suggestion systems, performance review, team-building activities, the use of survey data techniques, and many other contemporary management methods are basically efforts to identify and solve problems. But within each of these methodologies there is an implicit value orientation: problems get solved and jobs get done when people have an opportunity to express themselves and to have influence and impact on what is going on. Cutting people off just because they are angry or upset is a denial of this underlying psychological and organizational principle.

This does not mean that a manager, or an organization member, should stand still if he or she is being insulted or attacked. It does, however, strongly suggest that when one is receiving negative information, negative feedback, negative feelings from others, one can decrease the tension in the system—improve the relationship and problem-solving potential—by encouraging ventilation of tensions. It is equally true that just as other members of the system (subordinates, other departments, customers, other organizations) need an opportunity to have influence, to express themselves, to ventilate negative feelings, that you, too (as a manager or organization member), need an opportunity to express your feelings. One inappropriate conflict-resolution strategy is to assume that you are responsible for the feelings of others. That is, if other people are angry it is up to you to calm them down. If other people are unhappy it is up to you to make them happy. If people are inadequate it is up to you to make them adequate. The fact is that every person is ultimately responsible for his or her own behavior, his or her own career, his or her own effectiveness. Therefore, in dealing with conflict it is not necessary to demean yourself, to deny your own feelings, or to take responsibility for making other people feel good or feel effective. It is appropriate to encourage other people to express themselves, to show capacity to take in and respond to negative feedback, and to keep the system open. This can be done without in any way diminishing your self-respect or integrity, or your own psychological and organizational needs to express yourself, defend yourself, and have impact.

WHEN IN DOUBT: TRUST YOUR OWN FEELINGS

All of the techniques and formulations that have been presented in this and earlier chapters can be of value to you in building a larger repertoire of responses and increasing your capacity to deal with managerial and leadership problems. However, none of these methodologies can take the place of your own instincts, your own intuition, and your own natural capacities to deal with the world around you. The key issue is that as one learns, changes, grows, or becomes reinforced and more convinced of a particular pattern of behavior, the essential guideline is one's own internal feeling, one's intuition. The fact is that learning rarely occurs by denying or cutting off one's feelings. If one feels fear, anger, compassion, or affection, it is important to permit that feeling to surface, to experience it and use it as a way of dealing with the external world. For example, if you are attacked or unjustly and severely criticized or embarrassed by someone in higher authority, you may have a kind of socialized reaction; that is, you may remain calm and polite and perhaps even apologetic as the attack is going on, but you know, even as the attack occurs, that your real feeling is one of tension, resentment, and anger. It has been suggested several times throughout discussions of aggression and anger that the key issue is to take in and be aware of your own feelings. The point now is to go even further than being aware of those feelings, to trust them. If you feel anger, then the chances are good that you have a reason to feel angry. You are being put down, attacked, or in some fashion demeaned. Therefore, even as you employ enlightened techniques of conflict resolution it would be a serious mistake to get out of touch with your own feeling. Following is an example of how all of the strategies and points of view about change and behavior can be integrated as one responds to a difficult situation.

Assume your boss or someone in higher authority says: "You handled that problem inappropriately. You have cost the company a lot of money. I don't know how you could make such a stupid mistake."

From a theoretical point of view, based on the models presented earlier, the initial response to any kind of attack is to be Responsive first. Conversely, however, you have been urged not to deny your own feeling. One resolution of this dilemma is simply to express your feeling and to move it in a Responsive direction by saying something like: "I really don't understand how you can say that. What do you mean?"

Again, one need not stick to any given formulation in a robot-like manner but rather can decide to become Assertive immediately while still building in implicit responsiveness: "What you have said is, in my view, inaccurate and I find it very disturbing. There were good reasons for the course of action I took and I want us to talk about those reasons." These examples suggest that you can express your own feeling, you can acknowledge your own resentment and anger in dealing with conflict or disagreement, without, on the one hand, becoming overbearing, aggressive, and unreasonable or, on the other hand, becoming petulant and self-righteous. Here are some examples of behavior which may be tempting but rarely helps to solve problems—responses like the following:

"You have no right to talk to me that way."

"I've been doing a good job. Just who do you think you are?"

"Look, I'll stack myself up against anybody. I've been getting good results. Just because you are dissatisfied with one thing doesn't give you the right to attack me."

It is necessary, then, as you begin to work through conflict situations to recognize that conflict resolution involves an interdependent series of skills, insights, and capacities:

1. You can improve your conflict-resolution capacities by being more aware of the sources of your own behavior and by being more in touch with your own feelings.

2. You can improve your conflict-resolution capacities by being more aware of and more experienced with the alternatives that are available.

3. Finally, and most importantly, you can improve your interpersonal skills through practice and experience, thus tapping both your insight and awareness and your spontaneous capacities to deal with the surrounding environment.

Some Underlying Attitudes

In order for you to act effectively in a wide range of problem-solving and conflict situations which you encounter in organizational life, it is important to develop a supporting, underlying set of convictions or beliefs that are compatible with your past experience and that can be acted upon in day-to-day affairs. In summarizing conflict resolution and problem-solving strategies it is suggested that there are some predictable underlying orientations that are present, or will emerge, as you move toward a more fulfilling and effective leadership style. These orientation or belief systems are the focus of the next chapter.

10

The Future

MOVING AHEAD In human situations you never "have it made." Just when you think you understand your boss or your spouse or your friend, he or she does something unexpected. Just when you think you've got things under control, you find you have to respond to a new risk, a new challenge, a new emotional demand. The fact is that the idea of having it made is fatuous. The nature of the human situation in general, and of organizational life in particular, is that people are striving, changing, searching, competing in a social and physical environment that is also in flux. And so, although you in your leadership role must be steadfast, you can't be inflexible. Living systems—individuals, organizations, communities—are dynamic. Leadership styles, attitudes, and techniques that are static, that cause you to respond to the situations you face out of a predetermined set, simply won't work. Therefore, although there is a need for planning for the future, there is an even greater need for the development of the capacity to interact with a changing environment *now*.

Assertive-Responsive behavior is interactive. It is a way of dealing with the moment dynamically and realistically.

BELIEFS VERSUS BEHAVIOR When Assertive and Responsive patterns are integrated, you are then drawing upon your own internal resources *and* comprehending and responding to the world around you. Your ability to utilize what you have and to make appropriate, fulfilling choices in relating to others is in large measure determined by your basic values and beliefs. The bulk of this book has been aimed at defining, identifying, and analyzing leadership patterns which both theory and practical experience have proved valuable.

However, no amount of analysis, no well-intentioned plan, no set of procedures will work unless you act upon them.

Experiences and Feelings Conventional wisdom dictates that the thought is father—or, in our liberated world, father/mother—to the act. The fact is that action is energized by what you feel—sometimes responding by conscious thought, sometimes emerging spontaneously without much conscious thought—to an immediate stimulus. A less known and more important basis for understanding how your behavior changes is that new experiences bring to the surface new feelings—feelings that have been blocked or withheld—and new feelings often lead to the development of new beliefs and new patterns of behavior. Here, in capsule form we see how new experiences change old beliefs and create the opportunity for new modes of action.

Old belief: White soldier believes black soldier is irresponsible and cowardly. (Not O.K.)

New Experience: White and black soldiers have experiences together. They must work together, take risks with each other, help each other.

New feelings (white soldier toward black): Gratitude, affection, interdependence are some of the new feelings which may emerge: He helped me, I feel warm toward him. He was brave, I feel respect, etc.

New belief system: White soldier now believes this black soldier is brave and reliable. Depending on the past experiences and personality of the white soldier and on the intensity and nature of the new experience, a new belief system may emerge, such as:

All or most black soldiers are O.K.

This black soldier is O.K. I'm not sure about the others.

Black soldiers, like white soldiers, are individuals. Some are brave, some are not; some are more responsible than others.

New behaviors: With this new belief system the white soldier will behave differently with the black soldier. The white soldier may change his behavior toward all soldiers; he may be more open, treat people more as individuals, recognize some of his own prejudices, and redirect his own behavior. Note, too, that the black soldier may have gone through similar changes. He, too, may have started with a negative attitude and behaved antagonistically. Experience *may* change his beliefs and his behavior.

This basic process—developing new feelings as a result of new experiences and then developing new behaviors as a result of new beliefs—is at the core of personal growth. The changes that occur are not limited to how you feel about others, but influence the way you feel about yourself.

And so, by acting assertively and responsively, you may develop new beliefs, which, in turn, can lead to increased self-assertiveness and fulfillment. Clearly, an individual can act in ways which *do not* contribute to more effective new behavior. The aim of this book is to help you be aware of the options open to you, to have Assertive-Responsive skills at your fingertips, so that your chances of acting effectively are greatly enhanced. The manager who never behaves assertively will never open his/her self to the kind of new experiences which can create new belief systems and new and more effective behavior. In a kind of self-defeating circle, the manager who doesn't believe Assertive-Responsive behavior will work may never try it. And so if you wish to change and grow, you need to experiment with new behavior, you need to take risks. The first step in personal and managerial growth is knowing where you are. This book has urged you to assess yourself. The second step is to become aware of the options—techniques, procedures, alternatives—available to you. These options have been outlined in the Leadership Model. The third and most important step, which can occur even without the first two, is to act. Choose what you want to do and do it.

NEW BELIEF SYSTEMS　By finding new and more effective ways of acting you will develop new and more appropriate guidelines for yourself, that is, new belief systems. There is a set of beliefs, attitudes, and values most often associated with Assertive-Responsive leadership. Assertive and Responsive actions both support and are supported by these beliefs. If you find these beliefs consistent with where you choose to be, then it is also consistent to begin behaving assertively and responsively—now. Check over these beliefs and see where you stand.

I Believe

I can be supportive of the good feelings, integrity, and self-respect of others without diminishing my own good feelings, self-respect, or integrity.

I can pursue and protect my own rights without violating the rights of others.

I can be responsive to the needs, interests, and concerns of others while still maintaining my own convictions and integrity.

I can place demands (have a right to make demands) on others without diminishing or alienating them.

It is possible to compete with others without violating their rights.

It is possible to compromise and negotiate without violating my own rights.

It is possible and desirable to develop strategies and methods that assure that means and ends are compatible. I can be equally concerned with results and the means by which they come about.

Other people are unique and valuable.

Other people have the right to pursue their goals, to disagree with me, to defend their rights.

Acting on Your Beliefs Every leader, every organization member is concerned with converting his/her beliefs and aspirations into action. The final test of leadership effectiveness includes three elements:

1. Your behavior gets results.
2. You feel good about your behavior.
3. Your behavior contributes to the achievement of long-term goals and fulfilling relationships.

And so everyone wants to get somewhere and feel good as and when they get there. The most damaging assumption that you can make along the way is that somehow or other you must be perfect, you must be liked by everyone, you must be effective in every situation. Assertive-Responsive behavior is a reflection of the conviction that everyone needs to find ways of *reaching* the right answers, of *finding* improved situations. Most leaders, most innovators experience failure with surprising frequency; most new ideas encounter resistance and hostility. In practical terms, a realistic orientation toward work and interpersonal affairs is: "You never find a solution. You can only keep trying day by day."

Interpersonal and organizational effectiveness occur not because people fully understand each other or because they always do the right thing. Organizational and interpersonal effectiveness occur because people learn to deal with their own imperfections and the imperfections of others while striving for achievement. Assertive-Responsive behavior is built upon the conviction that people have the capacity to make things better and that organizational and personal effectiveness comes as a result of people striving for fulfillment while remaining open and vulnerable. When people act this way their behavior communicates a clear and important message: "I will risk letting you know what I think and feel; I will listen to you. I will risk being open and available; I will actively defend my rights. I will stand up for what I believe in; I will risk changing my mind. I am willing and able to learn from my own experience and from the experience of others."

CONCLUSION Everything is in the process of becoming something else. You are part of a changing organization, a changing world, a changing set of relationships. By making Assertive-Responsive choices you remain in touch with the core of your self and with the changing world around you. You shape the future not by what you do tomorrow; you shape the future by what you do now, today.

Appendix A

INTRODUCTION Many organization members have participated in Assertiveness programs that provide opportunities for individuals to get a better insight into their relationships with the manager to whom they report and with their subordinates. The reader may wish to ask his/her manager or subordinate to fill out an A & R Inventory so that he/she can compare that inventory with his/her own self-evaluation. Sample inventory forms follow for use in obtaining the manager's and subordinate's reaction to the reader's behavior.

The reader may also be interested in A & R Inventory data collected from approximately 1,000 managers. Data was collected regarding the manager's "self-image" and the way in which he/she perceived "The Boss."

1,000 Managers' Self-Image Scores

A Score <u>54.5</u>   R Score <u>65.5</u>

1,000 Managers' Perceptions of Their Boss

A Score <u>66.7</u>   R Score <u>53.3</u>

Note that the statistical averages show that most organization members see those in higher authority as being more Assertive than Responsive. Conversely, most managers see themselves as being slightly more Responsive than Assertive. There are notable exceptions to these averages and an analysis of the data shows that higher-level managers see themselves as being somewhat more Assertive than Responsive.

The following A & R Resources Inventories are reprinted by permission of Educational Systems and Designs, Inc., Westport, Conn., 1977.

A & R RESOURCES INVENTORY—THE SUBORDINATE

INSTRUCTIONS   Below you will find a series of paired statements, an "A" statement and an "R" statement. You are asked to distribute 10 points between the two statements. You might give all 10 points to the A statement and no points to the R statement. This would indicate that the A statement comes *closest* to describing your subordinate's behavior or feelings and the R statement is not at all descriptive. You might give equal points (5 points to A, 5 points to R) if both statements fit your subordinate's behavior about equally. (You might give 8 to A and 2 to R, or 4 to A and 6 to R, and so on.) For each question, A plus R should equal 10.

PAIRED STATEMENTS

A STATEMENTS	R STATEMENTS
1. My subordinate gets things done by shaping events, having a direct impact on people. Points _____	My subordinate gets things done by "tuning-in" on and responding to the people around him/her. Points _____
2. When my subordinate is dissatisfied with an individual's performance he/she becomes more demanding with the individual. My subordinate may make suggestions or set goals for improvement. Points _____	When my subordinate is dissatisfied with an individual's performance he/she observes, listens, and tries to understand the individual's behavior. My subordinate tries to involve him/her in setting goals. Points _____
3. If my subordinate errs in dealing with poor performance it is in the direction of being abrasive or resentful. (He/she might be seen as angry or hostile.) Points _____	If my subordinate errs in dealing with poor performance it is in the direction of accommodating or patronizing. (He/she might be seen as overly tolerant and compromising.) Points _____
4. In most group situations my subordinate is one of the people who initiates ideas, suggests alternatives, and energizes the process. Points _____	In most group situations my subordinate is one of the people who provides stability and balance. Responds to the ideas of others. Points _____
5. My subordinate gets results by using his/her own energy. Points _____	My subordinate gets results by tapping the energy of others. Points _____
6. My subordinate defends him/herself from attack or criticism by fighting back clearly and straightforwardly. My subordinate uses his/her energy to straighten things out. Points _____	My subordinate defends him/herself from attack or criticism by distracting or diffusing the energy of his/her opponent. Let's the other person tire him/herself out. Points _____

7. If my subordinate errs it is on the side of being too tough.

Points _____

   If my subordinate errs it is on the side of being too tolerant.

Points _____

8. When people disagree with one of my subordinate's ideas or suggestions he/she tends to "speed up" and try to sell them on his/her approach.

Points _____

   When people disagree with one of my subordinate's ideas or suggestions he/she tends to "slow down" and consider their reservations.

Points _____

9. My subordinate puts effort into being sure that people understand his/her point of view.

Points _____

   My subordinate puts effort into being sure that he/she understands the views of others.

Points _____

10. Under pressure my subordinate's strength lies in his/her ability to get "fired up" and to inspire others to act.

Points _____

   Under pressure my subordinate's strength lies in his/her ability to "take in" and remain open to the feelings of others.

Points _____

11. My subordinate's ability to be a strong competitor has paid off for him/her.

Points _____

   My subordinate's ability to be cooperative and to build collaborative relationships has paid off for him/her.

Points _____

12. My subordinate feels more comfortable talking than listening.

Points _____

   My subordinate feels more comfortable listening than talking.

Points _____

Total A points _____

Total R points _____

A & R RESOURCES INVENTORY—THE BOSS

INSTRUCTIONS   Below you will find a series of paired statements, an "A" statement and an "R" statement. You are asked to distribute 10 points between the two statements. You might give all 10 points to the A statement and no points to the R statement. This would indicate that the A statement comes *closest* to describing your boss's behavior or feelings and the R statement is not at all descriptive. You might give equal points (5 points to A, 5 points to R) if both statements fit his/her behavior about equally. (You might give 8 to A, and 2 to R, or 4 to A and 6 to R and so on.) For each question, A plus R should equal 10.

PAIRED STATEMENTS

A STATEMENTS	R STATEMENTS
1. My boss gets things done by shaping events, having a direct impact on people. Points _____	My boss gets things done by "tuning-in" on and responding to the people around him/her. Points _____
2. When my boss is dissatisfied with an individual's performance he/she becomes more demanding with the individual. My boss may make suggestions or set goals for improvement. Points _____	When my boss is dissatisfied with an individual's performance he/she observes, listens, and tries to understand the individual's behavior. My boss tries to involve him/her in setting goals. Points _____
3. If my boss errs in dealing with poor performance the error is in the direction of being abrasive or resentful. (He/she might be seen as angry or hostile.) Points _____	If my boss errs in dealing with poor performance the error is in the direction of accommodating or patronizing. (He/she might be seen as overly tolerant and compromising.) Points _____
4. In most group situations my boss is one of the people who initiates ideas, suggests alternatives, and energizes the process. Points _____	In most group situations my boss is one of the people who provides stability and balance. Responds to the ideas of others. Points _____
5. My boss gets results by using his/her own energy. Points _____	My boss gets results by tapping the energy of others. Points _____
6. My boss defends him/herself from attack or criticism by fighting back clearly and straightforwardly. My boss uses his/her energy to straighten things out. Points _____	My boss defends him/herself from attack or criticism by distracting or diffusing the energy of his/her opponent. He/she lets the other person tire him/herself out. Points _____

7. If my boss errs it is on the side of being too tough.

          Points _____

If my boss errs it is on the side of being too tolerant.

          Points _____

8. When people disagree with one of my boss's ideas or suggestions he/she tends to "speed up" and try to sell them on his/her approach.

          Points _____

When people disagree with one of my boss's ideas or suggestions he/she tends to "slow down" and consider their reservations.

          Points _____

9. My boss puts effort into being sure that people understand his/her point of view.

          Points _____

My boss puts effort into being sure that he/she understands the views of others.

          Points _____

10. Under pressure my boss's strength lies in his/her ability to get "fired up" and to inspire others to act.

          Points _____

Under pressure my boss's strength lies in his/her ability to "take in" and remain open to the feelings of others.

          Points _____

11. My boss's ability to be a strong competitor has paid off for him/her.

          Points _____

My boss's ability to be cooperative and to build collaborative relationships has paid off for him/her.

          Points _____

12. My boss feels more comfortable talking than listening.

          Points _____

My boss feels more comfortable listening than talking.

          Points _____

Total A points _____

Total R points _____

Appendix B

On the following pages you will find a series of training exercises designed to increase the individual's Assertive-Responsive skills. Many of these exercises can be tried out with co-workers or friends and are often included in Assertiveness Training programs for managers. (All the exercises are copyrighted by Educational Systems and Designs, Inc., and are reprinted by permission.)

ASSERTIVE STYLES

OBJECTIVES
1. To become familiar with various styles of assertion.
2. To identify styles based on verbal and written presentation.
3. To construct responses in the various categories of assertion.

PROCEDURE
The following steps will be completed by all groups together in a general session.

Step 1:   Review the Assertive styles that follow.

Step 2:   Then you will find an exchange between a supervisor and subordinate. Identify each of the responses in terms of the styles previously reveiwed.

Step 3:   Finally, you will find several problem situations. Prepare an Assertive response for each of these problems.

ASSERTIVE STATEMENT STYLES

ASSERTIVE-RESPONSIVE
A straight message of where you are (attitude, perception, need) and a request for the other's opinion (feeling, etc.).

> I want to leave early to take my son to the doctor. Would that leave you short-handed?

> I think the work force should be reduced. What's your opinion?

EMPATHETIC ASSERTION
A statement that uses both empathy and assertion. (Some recognition of the other's situation plus statement of your want.)

> I see you're busy. I need five minutes of your time.

> I know the market is tight and competition is getting tougher. However, I feel that sales can be increased.

SIMPLE ASSERTION A simple statement that gives information, states a position, and shows that one stands up for one's rights.

> I can't hear you.

> Costs were 10 percent over the budget this quarter.

DISCREPANCY ASSERTION A statement of the discrepancy followed by your want. Points out the discrepancy between what a person says and does.

> I understood from our last talk that I was to get a raise this month. I haven't received it and I'd like to know what happened.

NEGATIVE FEELING ASSERTION A descriptive statement of your self-interest made when your rights are being violated. It includes (1) your feelings, the other's behavior, and your preference, or (2) your feelings, the other's behavior, and the concrete effect.

1. "I feel _____ when you _____ and I'd like you to _____ ."

    Example: I feel uncomfortable and at times resentful when you criticize me at a staff meeting. I'd like you to give me negative feedback in private.

2. "I feel (*describe feeling*) when you (*describe situation or behavior*) because (*how it affects your life in a concrete way*)."

    Example: I feel resentful when you criticize me at a meeting because it makes me look bad in the eyes of my peers.

COMPROMISE ASSERTION A statement that expresses a willingness to compromise in the interests of moving toward a goal. It reflects a truthful and sensitive readiness to reach agreement, usually after one has asserted oneself.

> I can accept that idea, although I would be happier with the other.

ASSERTIVE STYLES PRACTICE

A Discussion of Performance

1. *Supervisor:* I asked you to come in today to review your performance on some of your departmental goals.
    Identify: _____

2. *Subordinate:* I'm glad to be here. From our last conversation I gathered we were going to try to get together on this about once a week. We

haven't done that and I'd like to get back to a once-a-week review on pressing issues.

Identify: _____

3. *Supervisor:* Well, I can certainly understand that. I realize that you and I would both like to look at these things more frequently. However, I feel we have to respond to changing situations. I'd like us to be able to schedule some regular meetings but also have the flexibility to change our schedule as situations change.

Identify: _____

4. *Subordinate:* I see. Well, I suggest we have a regularly scheduled session about once a month and get together as needed on hot issues. Does that sound appropriate to you?

Identify: _____

5. *Supervisor:* Sure, I can go along with that. I do have something of a preference for simply getting together as needed, but let's agree that we'll meet once a month in any case.

Identify: _____

Performance Review, Stage Two

1. *Supervisor:* I've noted that output in your department is about 10 percent lower than we had originally targeted. I'd like to see that gap closed.

Identify: _____

2. *Subordinate:* I think I could get better results if we reallocated some of our budget commitments. Is that possible?

Identify: _____

3. *Supervisor:* I can certainly understand your desire to modify the budget. I know there have been a lot of operational changes caused by new kinds of sales activity. I'd like to work toward stabilizing the line budget on a quarterly basis at least, rather than modifying it when selling activities change.

Identify: _____

4. *Subordinate:* In our last discussion it seems we agreed that my goal was to stay within the program budget allocations, and that some shift in line items would be okay. But in some of our recent conversations it appears that you're holding me to a line budget which, in my opinion, is not what we agreed to. I feel that if program budget items are on target then that is evidence of effective budgetary controls.

Identify: _____

ANSWER KEY

A Discussion of Performance	Performance Review, Stage Two
1. Simple Assertion	1. Simple Assertion
2. Discrepancy Assertion	2. Assertive-Responsive
3. Empathetic Assertion	3. Empathetic Assertion
4. Assertive-Responsive	4. Discrepancy Assertion
5. Compromise Assertion	

PROBLEMS Here are three problem situations. Design one of the Assertive responses.

Problem I: A subordinate comes to you complaining that he/she was promised more responsibility and hasn't gotten it. Your view is that the promise was "two-edged." The subordinate had made a commitment to develop some new programs and thereby demonstrate the capacity to assume more responsibility. The programs have not been developed. Your response when he/she complains is:

_____

_____

_____

_____

_____

Problem II: The boss calls you in and criticizes you for spending too much time working with your subordinates in small groups. He/she says, "You just seem to be meeting happy. Why don't you get your people out doing some work?" Your own feeling is that (a) you have been producing better results over the last six months than prior supervisors in this same position, and (b) your subordinates are meeting quality and quantity of work expectations. Design a response.

_____

_____

_____

_____

Problem III: A customer or client says to you, "I know you can shave corners on this and I don't mind if you get a little personal gain or improve your status, but you'll have to give me a break if you want my cooperation." Design a response.

_____

_____

_____

_____

_____

CHOICES

OBJECTIVE   To reinforce the idea that each of us has a choice about what we do.

PROCEDURE   *Step 1:*   List 5 or 6 items on the left side of the following form that you feel you *must* do when you return to work.

Step 2:   Working in pairs, express each of the items on your list to your partner. Start each statement with the words, "I must"; e.g., "I must speak to my boss about increasing staff." When number 1 has finished his/her list, number 2 goes through his/her list in the same manner.

Step 3:   Number 1 will now go through the *same* list of items. However, this time he/she will use the words, "I choose"; e.g., "I choose to speak to my boss about increasing staff." Again, when 1 has completed the list, 2 goes through his/her list.

CHOICES

I Must:

BEHAVIOR REHEARSAL AND APPLICATION

OBJECTIVES
1. To apply Assertive behavior in a specific and realistic situation.
2. To get feedback and discuss back-home application of Assertive behavior.

PROCEDURE
Step 1: Identify a face-to-face situation in which you feel it is desirable to be Assertive, possibly one about which you have been uncomfortable in the past or one which you anticipate with apprehension. It should be specific and "individual centered," perhaps a performance review, a disciplinary action, or an interdepartmental disagreement. Choose a situation in which you feel you can accomplish your objectives by being Assertive. Here's the sequence of the process.

a) Situation: Format I

Make some notes on the following components of the situation.

- Background: Who is involved? What's the situation? (Make this as brief as possible.)
- Objective: What do you want to achieve in this situation?

b) Planning Notes: Format II

- What ideas or suggestions have you received so far?
- What do you want to maintain?
- What do you want to improve or change?

BEHAVIOR REHEARSAL SITUATION FORMAT I

a) *Background*

b) *My objective*

Step 2:   Meet in a group of five and start by assigning numbers to each group member, 1, 2, 3, 4, and 5. The balance of these instructions refers to parts played by each individual in the first sequence. However, each sequence is repeated for each individual in the group.

a) Number 1 describes the situation briefly. Number 1 faces 2 and presents his/her assertive statement(s) (2 does not respond). Other members arrange themselves so that they can observe 1's presentation.

b) Each group member then gives positive (P) feedback to 1; i.e., they tell 1 what they liked about the statement(s), what positive result they would expect.

c) Number 1 listens to positive feedback from each member and then identifies what he/she might wish to change in the statement(s) in the next sequence. Number 1 self-corrects (S).

d) Each member now gives improvement (I) feedback. In what ways might it not achieve 1's purpose? How could it be improved?

e) Number 1 now modifies the statement(s) and faces 3 and presents his/her modified response (3 remains silent).

f) The feedback sequence is repeated (P, S, I).

g) Now 1 identifies the ways in which the other person in the actual situation usually resists, hassles, or is unresponsive to 1's attempts to produce results. So, 1 should try to describe what the other person says or does that blocks him/her, that makes it hard for him/her to come across, that arouses fear, guilt, anger, etc?

h) Number 1 now presents a modified assertive statement to 4. However, in this instance 4 does not remain silent after the statement but utilizes the information provided by 1 in Step (g) to hassle, resist, or in some fashion block 1 from achieving his/her desired purpose.

i) Number 1 now responds assertively to this hassle.

j) The feedback sequence is repeated, covering both the original Assertive statement and the response to the hassle.

k) Number 1 now repeats the cycle one final time with 5 who hassles after the initial statement(s). Feedback (P, S, I) is given in turn, covering both the initial statement and the response to the hassle.

Step 3:   Rotate the numbers so that 2 moves up to become 1, 3 becomes 2, and so forth. Repeat Step 2. Afterwards rotate the numbers again until each member of the group has completed the Step 2 cycle.

Try to use your Planning Format and notes so that you *practice* those specific skills which feedback and observation have identified as being most useful for you.

BEHAVIOR REHEARSAL PLANNING FORMAT II

1. Identify suggestions from feedback or observation which you can apply to behavior rehearsal:

    _____

    _____

    _____

2. Identify behavioral goals for the upcoming rehearsal.

	SAME	Check MORE	LESS
Clarity of objectives	———	———	———
Express wants	———	———	———
Eye contact	———	———	———
Voice volume	———	———	———
Forcefulness	———	———	———
Listening	———	———	———
Clear and specific	———	———	———
Concise	———	———	———
Seek out others' opinions	———	———	———
Friendly	———	———	———
Responsive	———	———	———
Candid	———	———	———

    Add your own summary or additional goals:

    _____

    _____

    _____

REHEARSAL STEPS

With a 4-person team

a) 2 "cues" 1 (and then is silent)

    1 responds assertively to 2

    2, 3, 4 give feedback (P, S, I)

b) 3 cues 1 in the same manner

    1 responds assertively to 3

    2, 3, 4 give feedback (P, S, I)

With a 5-person team

a) 2 cues 1 (and then is silent)

    1 responds assertively to 2

    2 does not respond

    2, 3, 4, 5 give feedback (P, S, I)

b) 3 cues 1 in the same manner

    1 responds assertively to 3

    3 does not respond

    2, 3, 4, 5 give feedback (P, S, I)

c) 4 cues 1

   1 responds to 4

   4 hassles, i.e., does not accept the assertion

   1 responds assertively

   2, 3, 4 give feedback (P, S, I)

d) 2 cues 1 again

   1 responds assertively

   2 hassles

   1 responds assertively

   2, 3, 4 give feedback (P, S, I)

c) 4 cues 1

   1 responds assertively to 4

   4 hassles (does not accept the assertion)

   1 responds assertively

   2, 3, 4, 5 give feedback (P, S, I)

d) 5 cues 1

   1 responds assertively to 5

   5 hassles

   1 responds assertively

   2, 3, 4, 5 give feedback (P, S, I)

ASSERTIVE-RESPONSIVE CLUES

VERBAL
- Intent is to communicate.
- Not putting self or others down.
- Firm but not hostile.
- Direct and to the point.
- "Want" is stated or reflected.
- Shows some consideration for the other.
- Leaves room for escalation.
- If an explanation, short and without excuses.
- No blaming, pleading, sarcasm, whining.
- Feelings discussed; shared; check out profanity.
- Words are real and authentic.

NONVERBAL
Congruency
- Eye contact (not staring or glaring).
- Straight body stance.
- Appropriate facial expressions.
- Hands (not pleading or threatening gestures).
- Voice: appropriate volume and pitch; not harsh, raspy, whiney.

FEEDBACK (P, S, I)
P Team starts with strengths. In what ways was the presenter Assertive?
S Presenter tells what he/she would change to be more Assertive.
I Team now suggests possible changes to be more Assertive.

HINTS FOR FEEDBACK
1. *Describe*, don't judge or label.
2. Offer *concrete* suggestions.
3. Offer *possible* ways to change.
4. Leave room for presenter to accept, refuse, or modify the suggestion.